FOR ORGANS, PIANOS & ELECTRONIC KEYBOARDS

**EZ PLAY TODAY**

**184**

# MERLE HAGGARD
## ANTHOLOGY
### OVER 45 OF HIS BEST HITS

T0084008

## CONTENTS

**HAL•LEONARD®**
CORPORATION

7777 W. BLUEMOUND RD. P.O. BOX 13819 MILWAUKEE, WI 53213

# Are The Good Times Really Over For Good

Registration 5
Rhythm: Waltz

Words and Music by
Merle Haggard

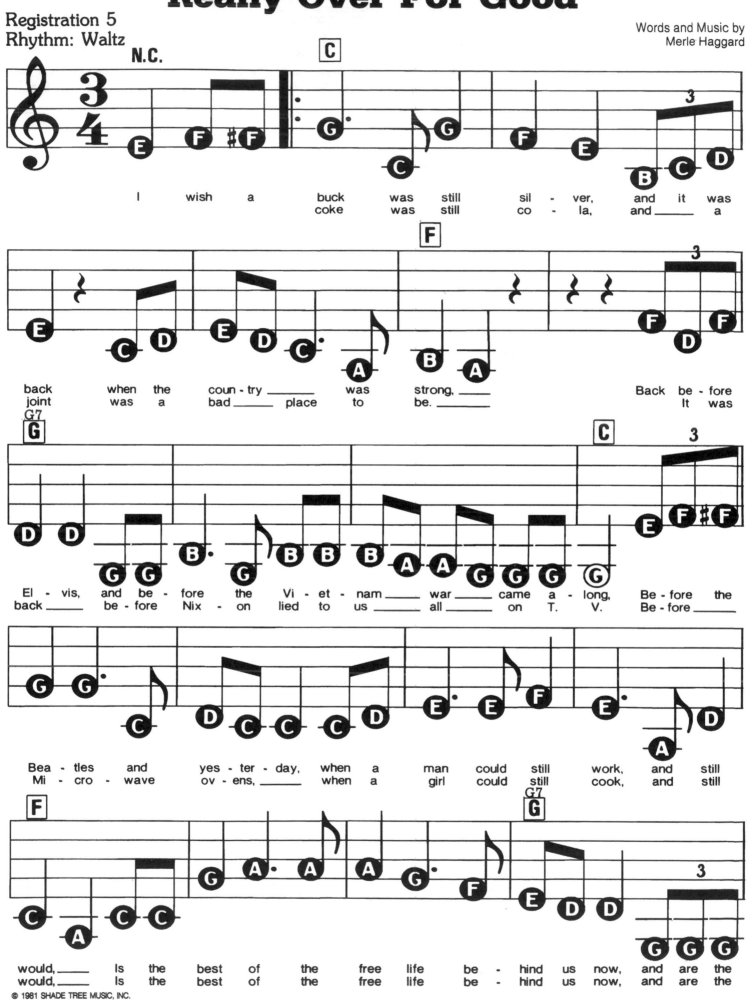

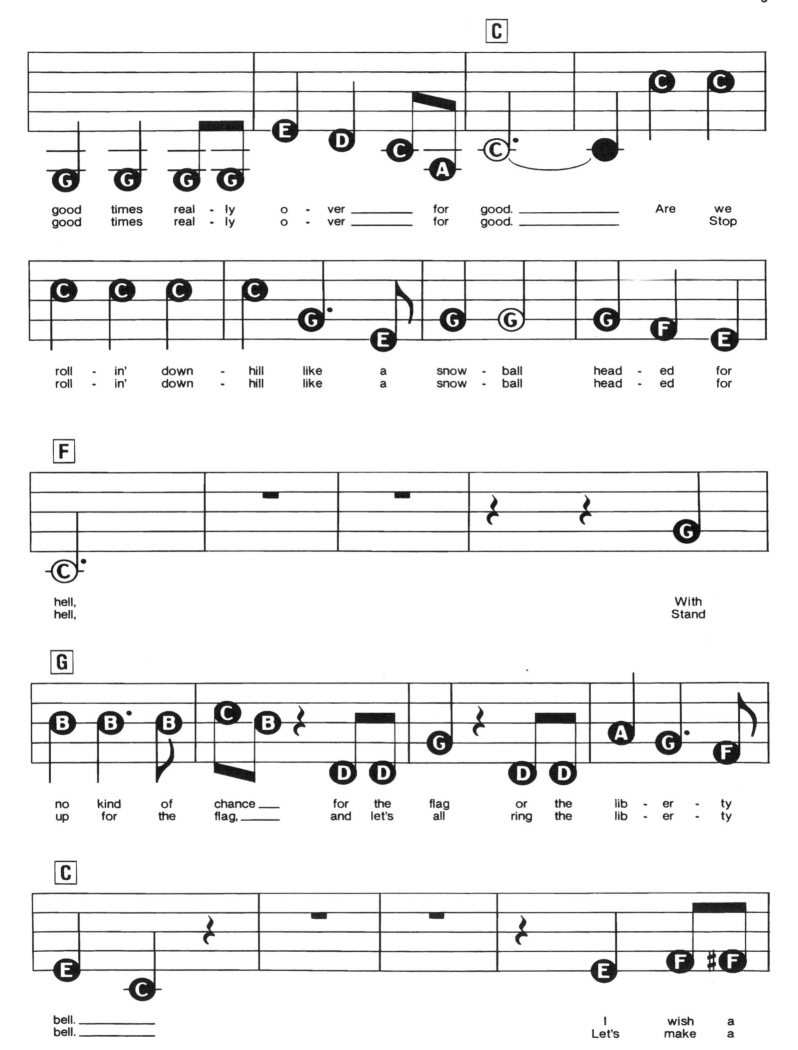

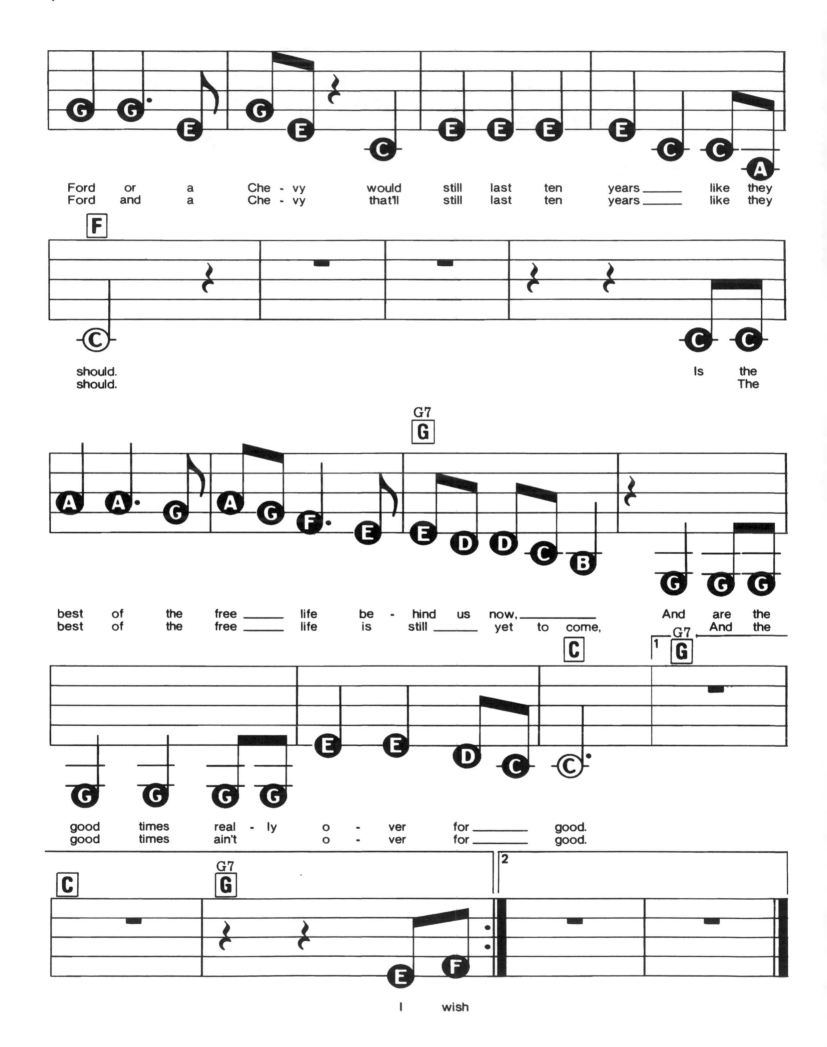

# Big City

Registration 2
Rhythm: Shuffle

Words and Music by
Merle Haggard and Dean Holloway

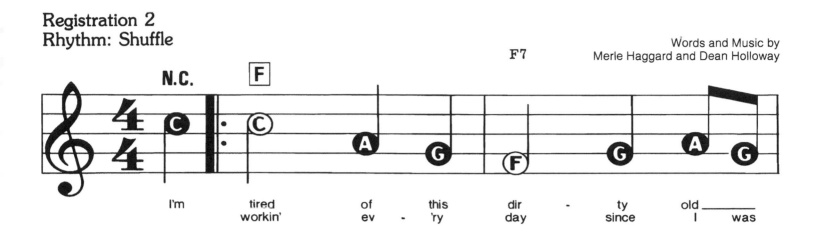

I'm    tired    of    this    dir - ty    old ____
workin'    ev - 'ry    day    since    I    was

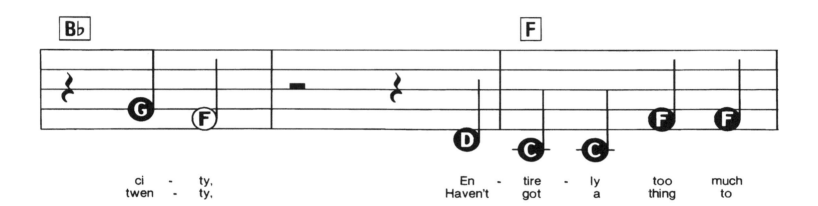

ci - ty,    En - tire - ly    too    much
twen - ty,    Haven't    got    a    thing    to

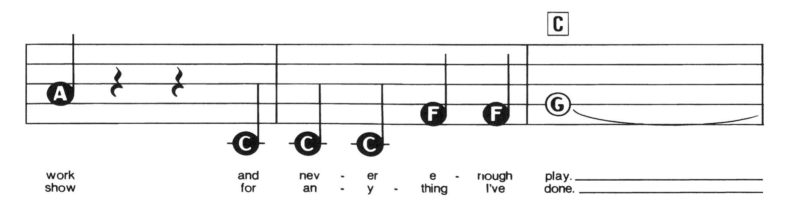

work    and    nev - er    e - nough    play. ____
show    for    an - y - thing    I've    done. ____

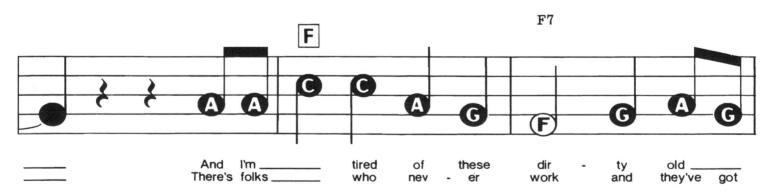

____    And    I'm ____    tired    of    these    dir - ty    old ____
There's    folks ____    who    nev - er    work    and    they've    got

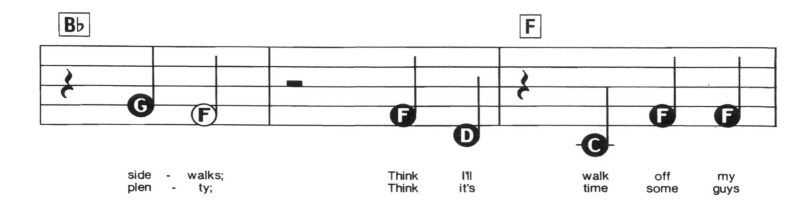

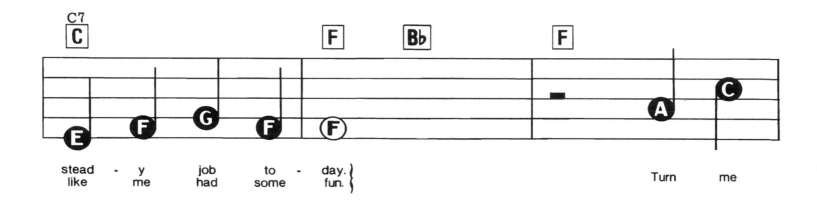

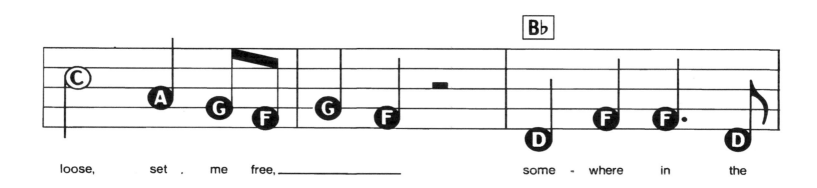

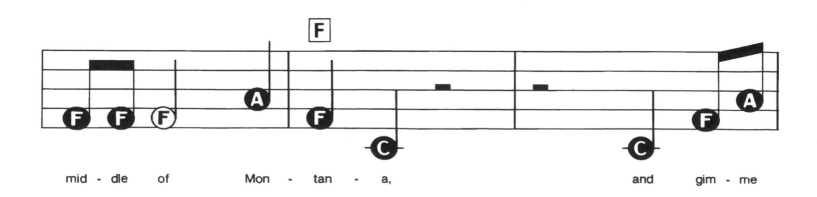

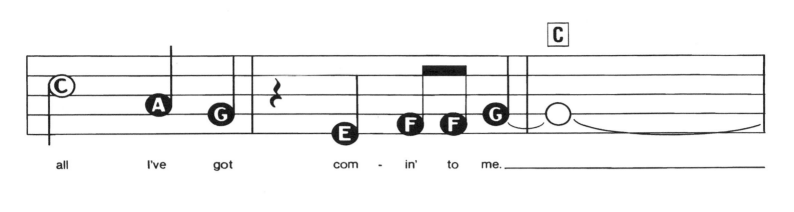

all I've got com - in' to me. _____

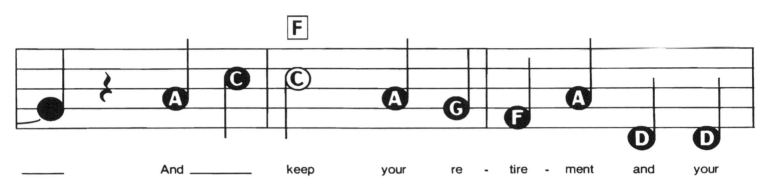

_____ And _____ keep your re - tire - ment and your

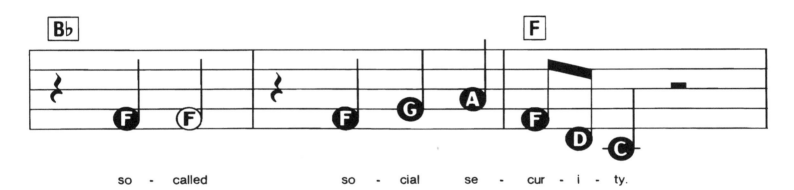

so - called so - cial se - cur - i - ty.

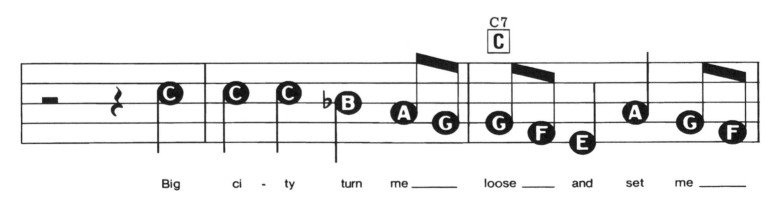

Big ci - ty turn me _____ loose _____ and set me _____

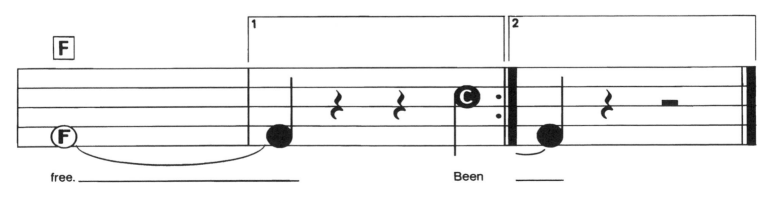

free. _____ Been _____

# The Bottle Let Me Down

Registration 3
Rhythm: Country or Shuffle

Words and Music by
Merle Haggard

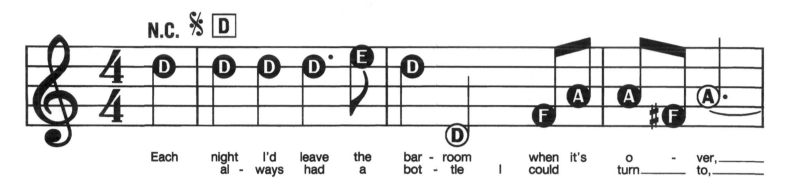

Each night I'd leave the bar - room when it's o - ver,_____
al - ways had a bot - tle I could turn_____ to,_____

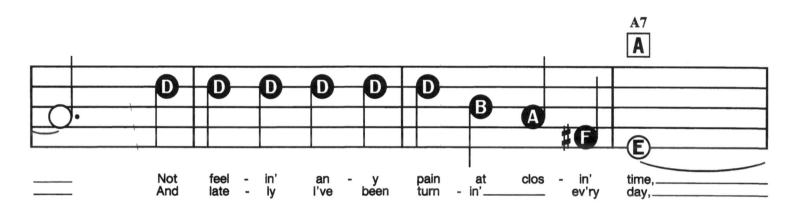

_____ Not feel - in' an - y pain at clos - in' time,_____
_____ And late - ly I've been turn - in'_____ ev'ry day,_____

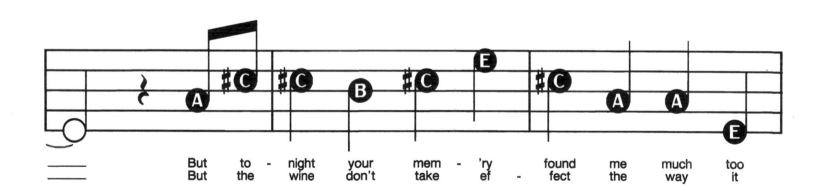

_____ But to - night your mem - 'ry found me much too
_____ But the wine don't take ef - fect the way it

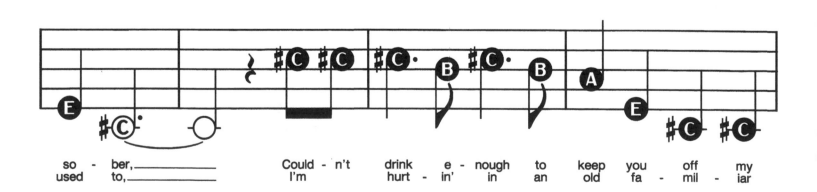

so - ber,_____ Could - n't drink e - nough to keep you off my
used to,_____ I'm hurt - in' in an old fa - mil - iar

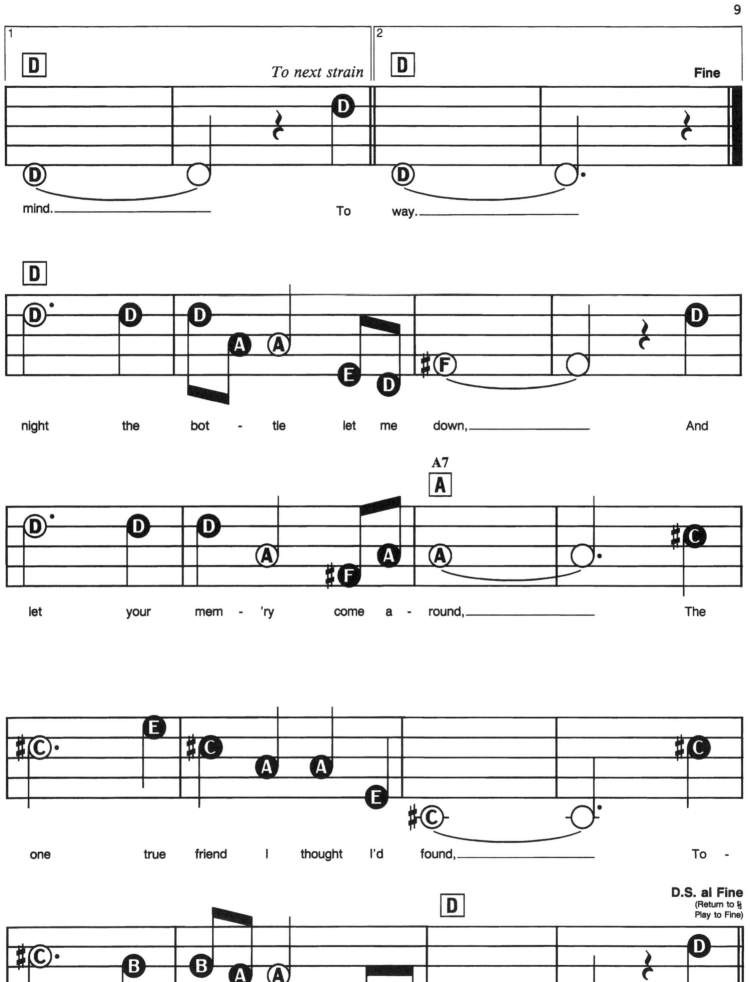

# Branded Man

Registration 2
Rhythm: Country or Shuffle

Words and Music by
Merle Haggard

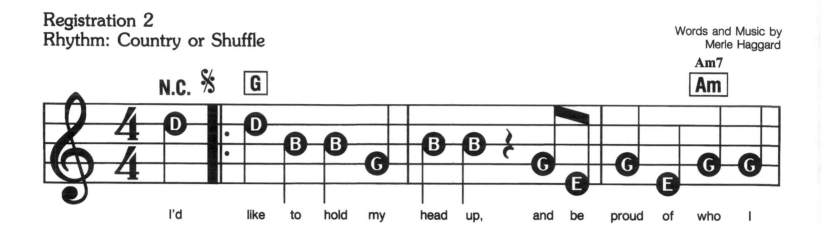

I'd like to hold my head up, and be proud of who I

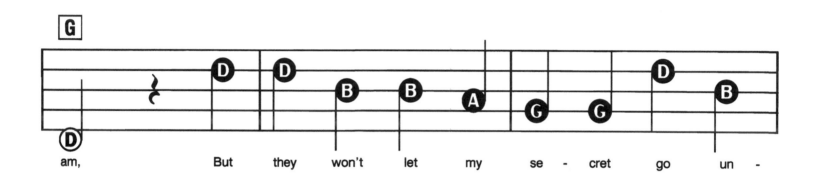

am, But they won't let my se - cret go un -

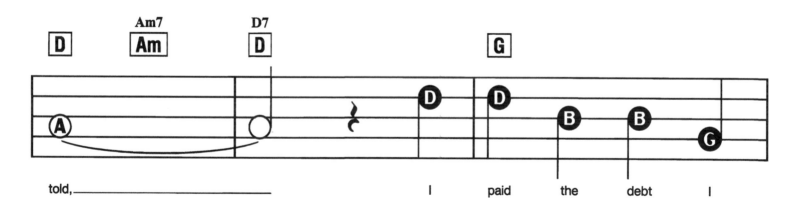

told,_____ I paid the debt I

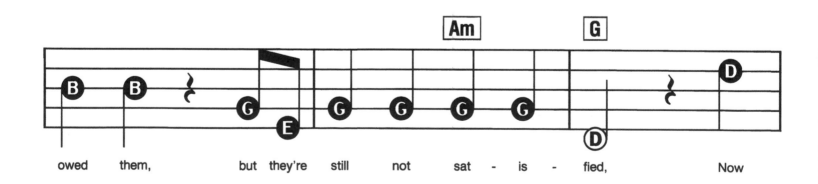

owed them, but they're still not sat - is - fied, Now

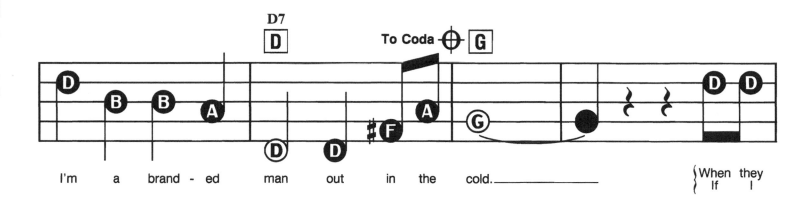

I'm a brand - ed man out in the cold._____ When they
If I

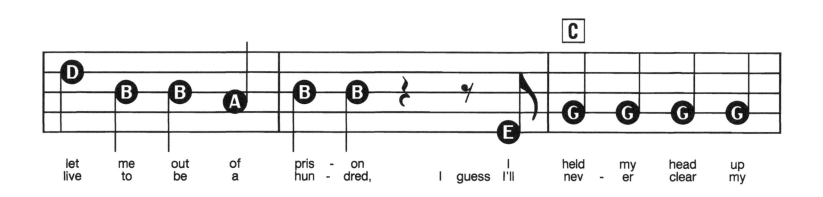

let me out of a pris - on I held my head up
live to be a hun - dred, I guess I'll nev - er clear my

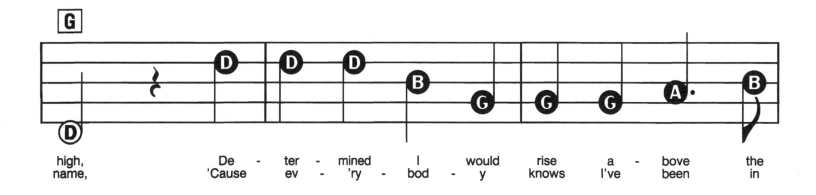

high, De - ter - mined I would rise a - bove the
name, 'Cause ev - 'ry - bod - y knows I've been the in

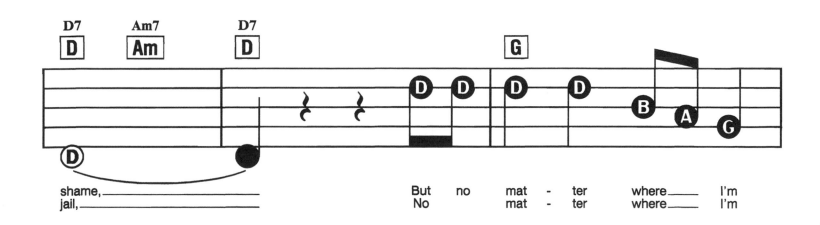

shame,_____ But no mat - ter where_____ I'm
jail,_____ No mat - ter where_____ I'm

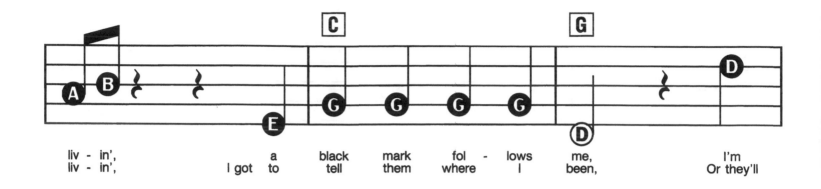

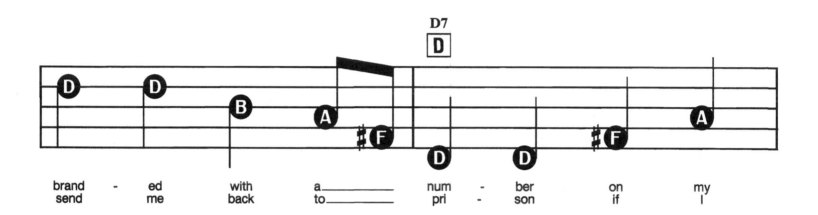

liv - in',     I got a black mark fol - lows me,     I'm
liv - in',     I got to tell them where I been,     Or they'll

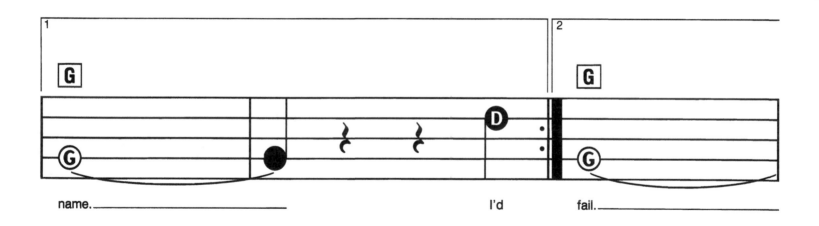

brand - ed with a_____ num - ber on my
send me back to_____ pri - son if I

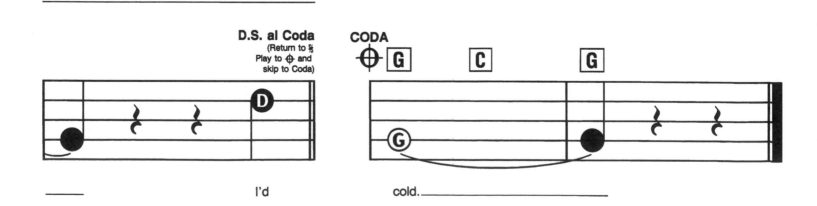

name._____     I'd fail._____

**D.S. al Coda**
(Return to 𝄋
Play to ⊕ and
skip to Coda)

**CODA**

_____ I'd cold._____

# Carolyn

**Registration 1**
**Rhythm: Country or Shuffle**

Words and Music by
Tommy Collins

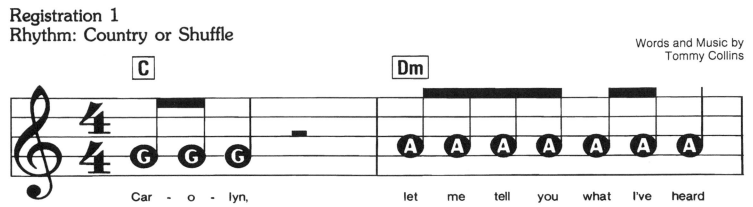

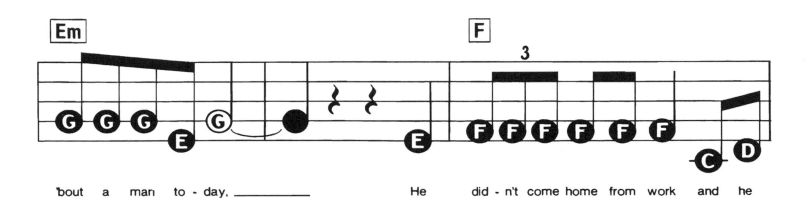

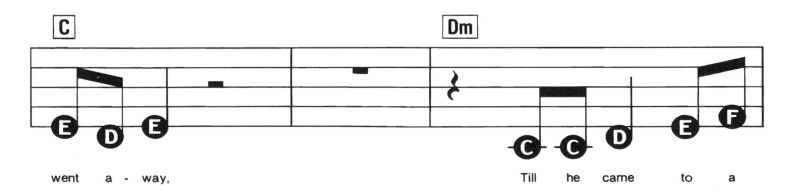

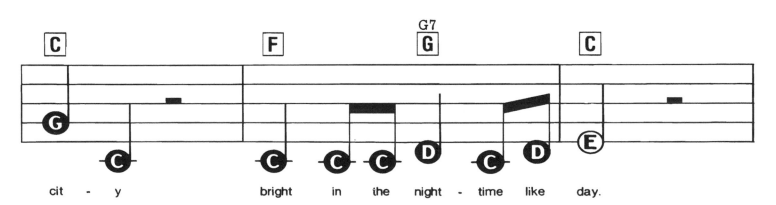

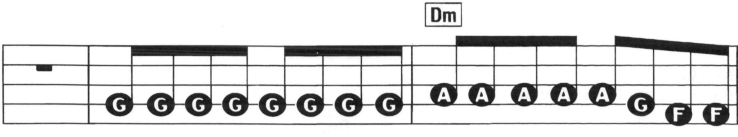

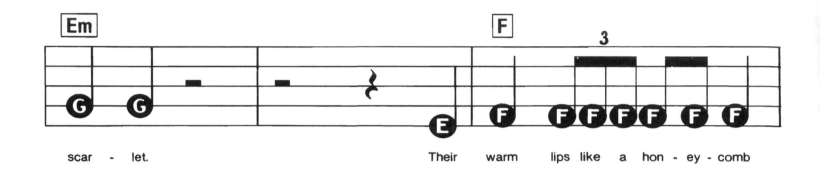

There they say he met up with some wom-en dressed in yel - low and

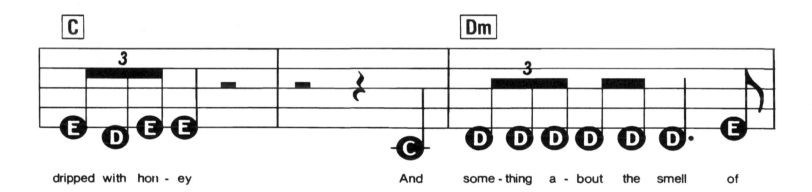

scar - let. Their warm lips like a hon-ey-comb

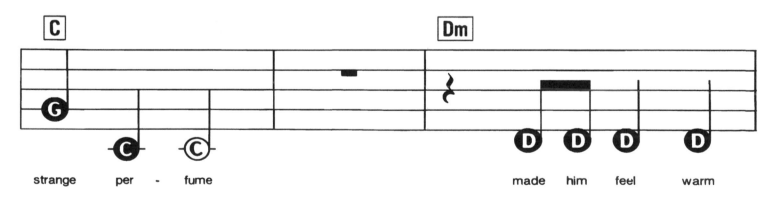

dripped with hon-ey And some-thing a-bout the smell of

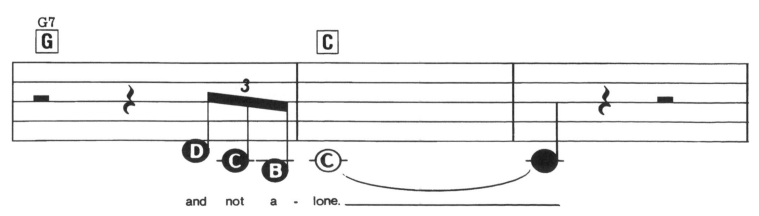

strange per - fume made him feel warm

and not a - lone.

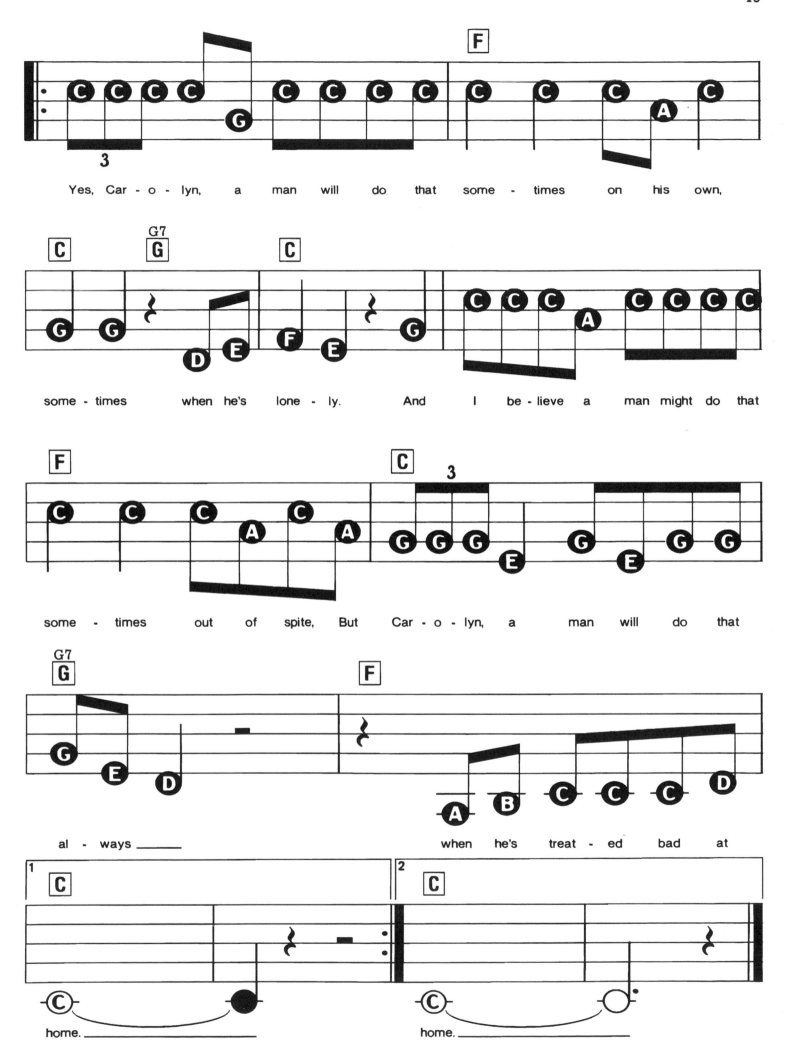

# Daddy Frank
## (The Guitar Man)

Registration 4
Rhythm: Country or Shuffle

Words and Music by
Merle Haggard

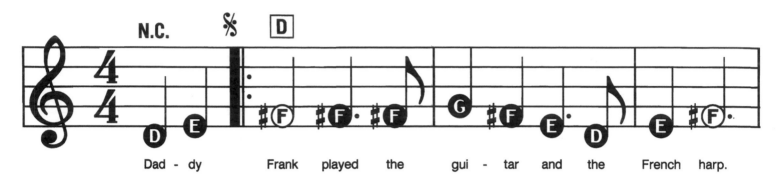

Dad - dy Frank played the gui - tar and the French harp.

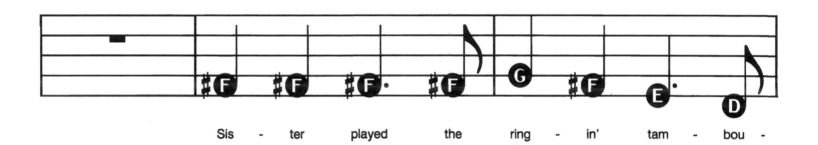

Sis - ter played the ring - in' tam - bou -

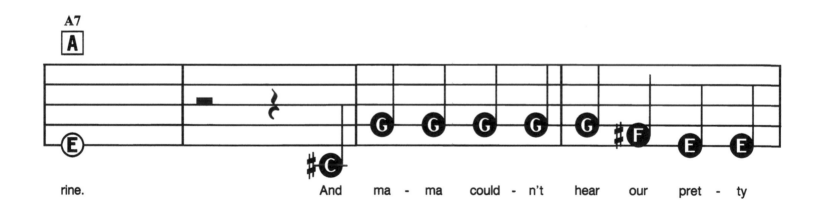

rine. And ma - ma could - n't hear our pret - ty

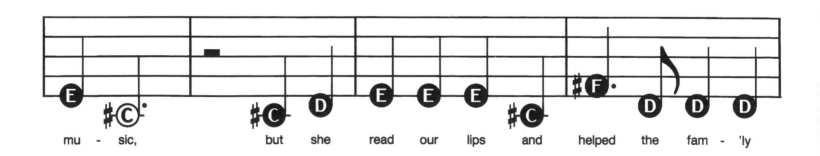

mu - sic, but she read our lips and helped the fam - 'ly

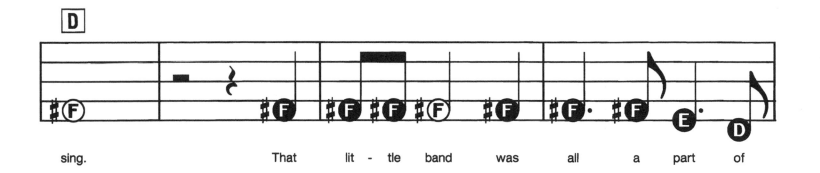

sing.    That   lit - tle   band   was   all   a   part   of

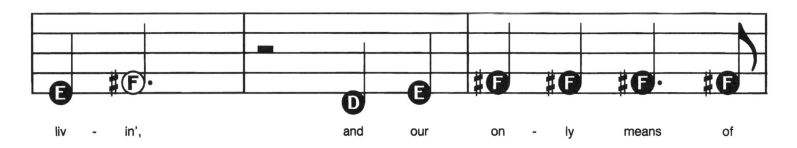

liv - in',     and   our   on - ly   means   of

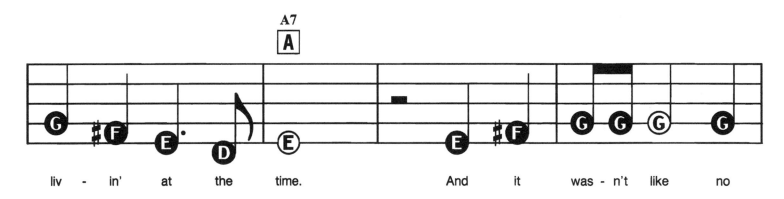

liv - in'  at  the  time.    And   it   was - n't  like  no

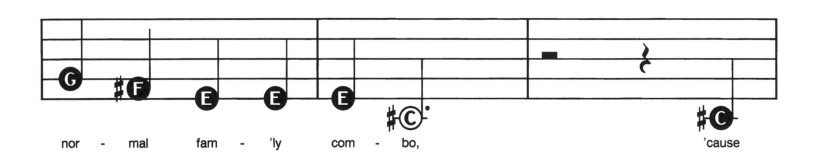

nor - mal  fam - 'ly  com - bo,      'cause

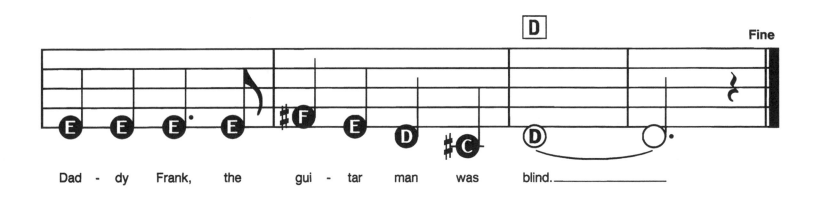

Dad - dy   Frank,   the   gui - tar  man  was   blind._____

19

# Everybody's Had The Blues

Registration 9
Rhythm: Swing or Shuffle

Words and Music by
Merle Haggard

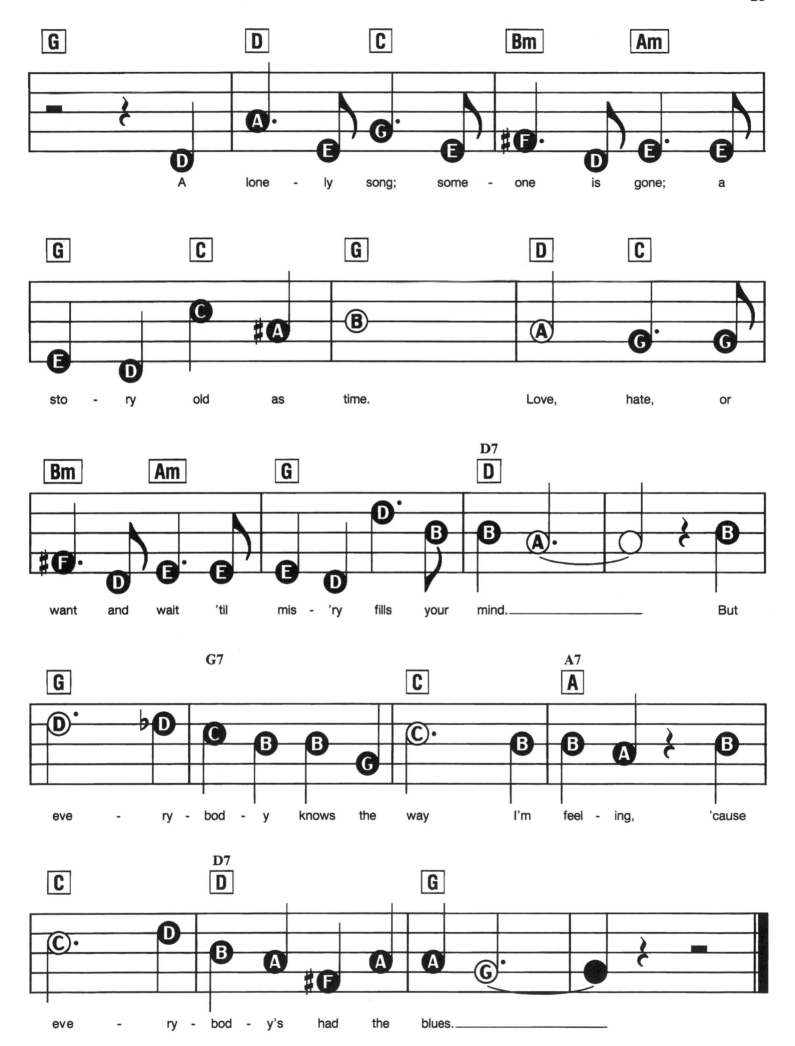

# The Emptiest Arms In The World

Registration 10
Rhythm: Country Western

Words and Music by
Merle Haggard

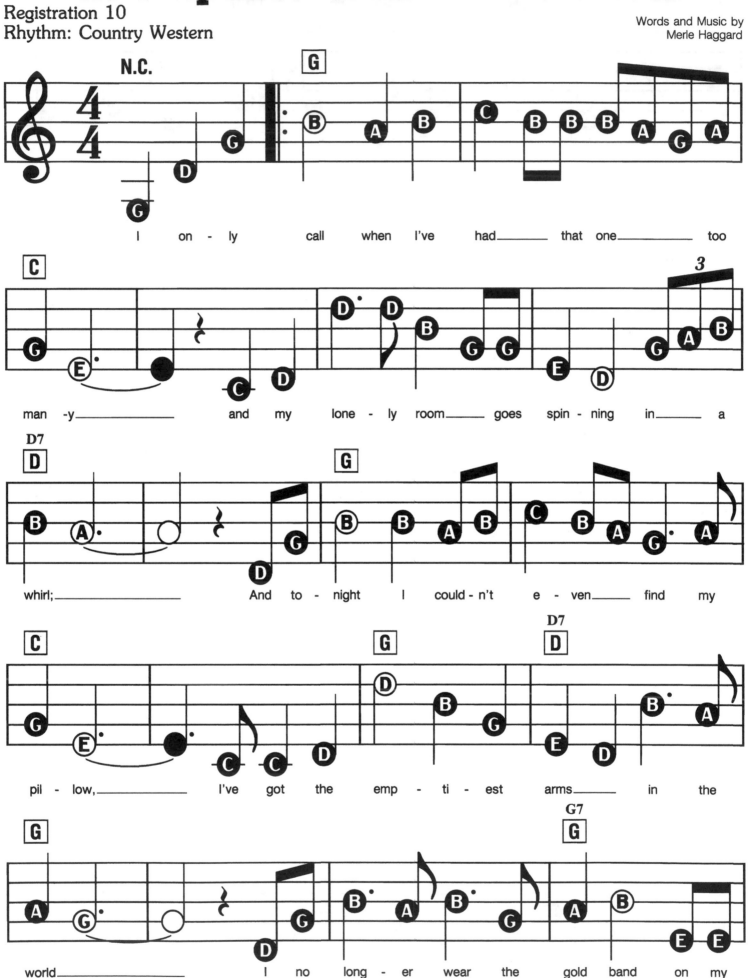

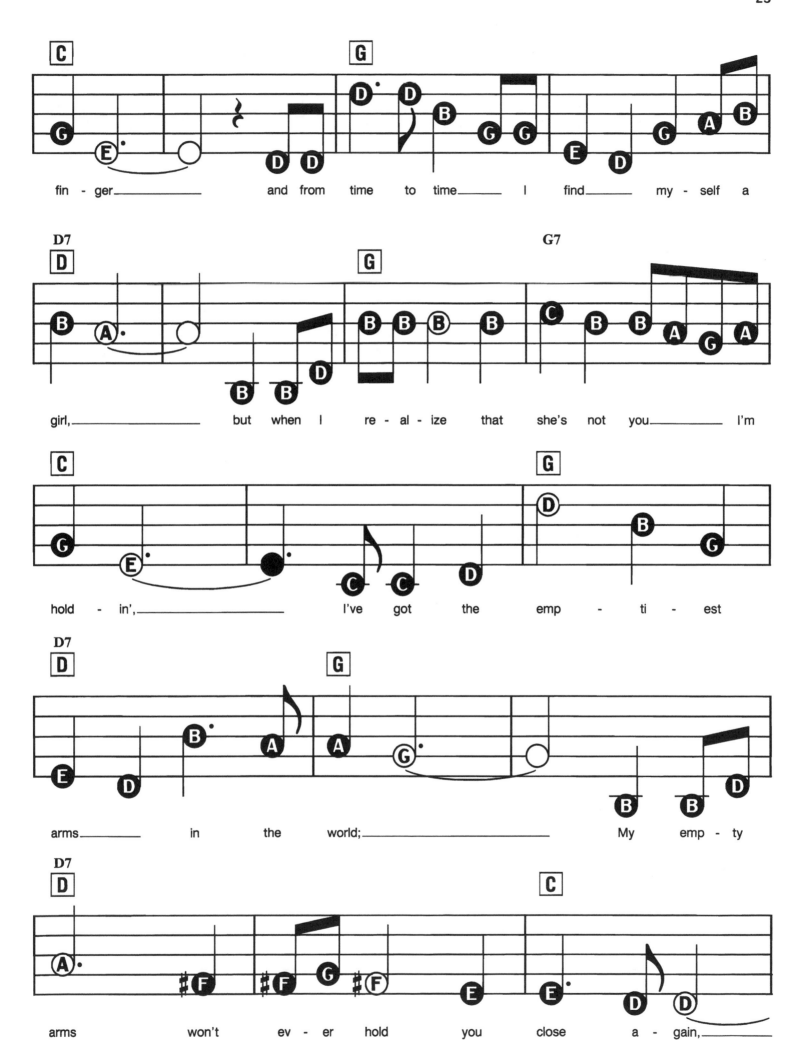

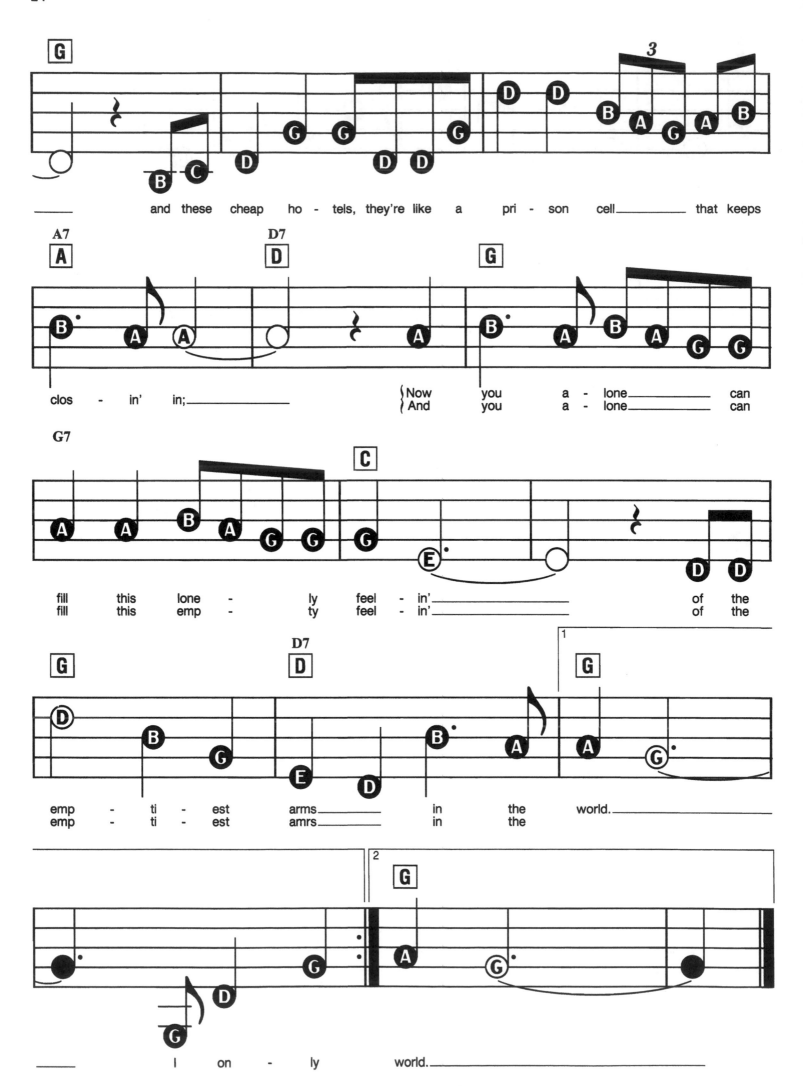

# Going Where The Lonely Go

Registration 10
Rhythm: Rock or 8 Beat

Words and Music by
Merle Haggard and Dean Holloway

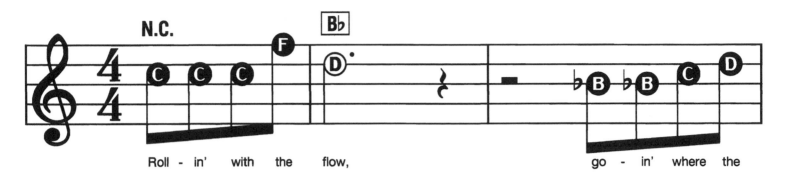

Roll - in' with the flow, go - in' where the

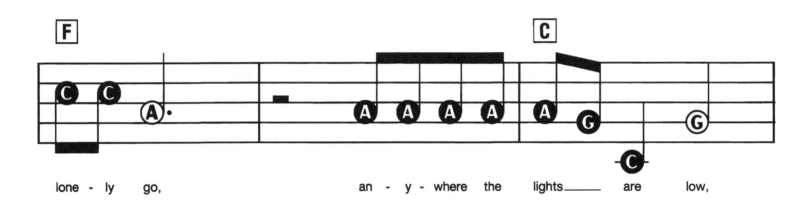

lone - ly go, an - y - where the lights___ are low,

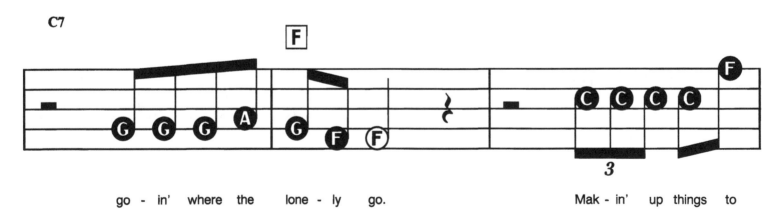

go - in' where the lone - ly go. Mak - in' up things to

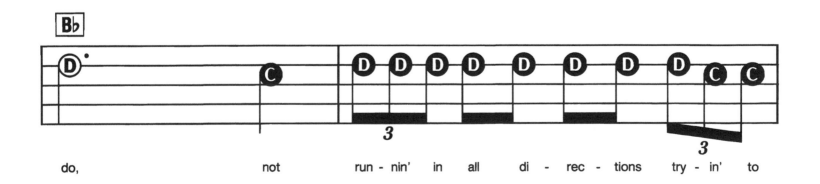

do, not run - nin' in all di - rec - tions try - in' to

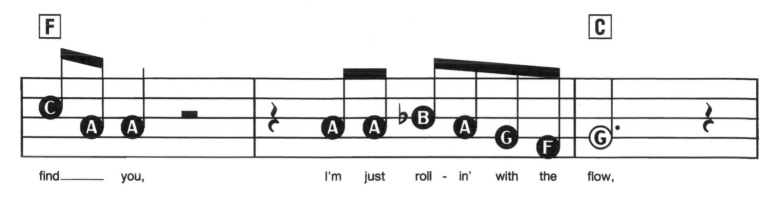

find_____ you,     I'm just roll - in' with the     flow,

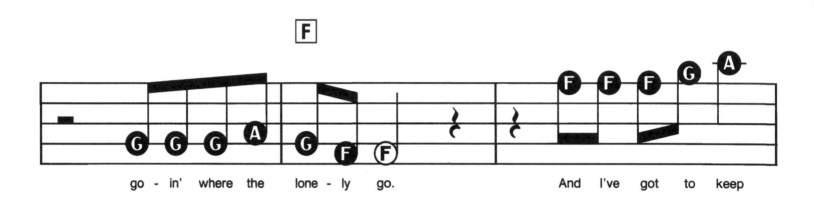

go - in' where the   lone - ly   go.          And I've got to keep

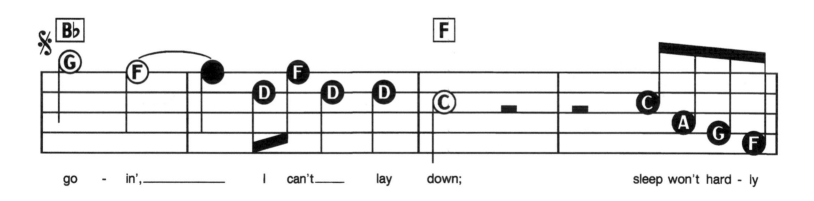

go - in',_____ I can't____ lay   down;          sleep won't hard - ly

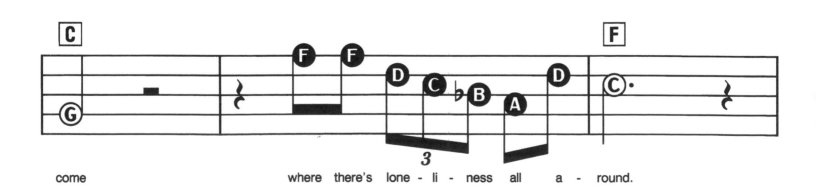

come          where there's lone - li - ness all a - round.

27

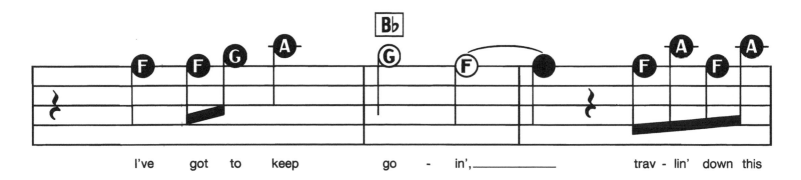

I've got to keep go - in',_____ trav - lin' down this

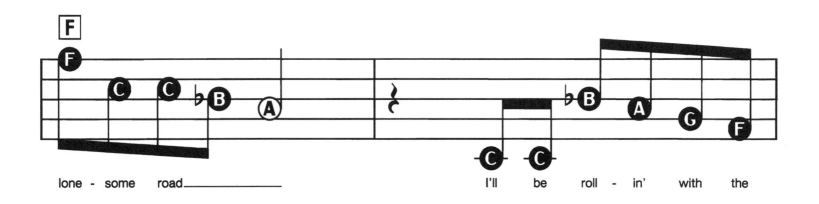

lone - some road_____ I'll be roll - in' with the

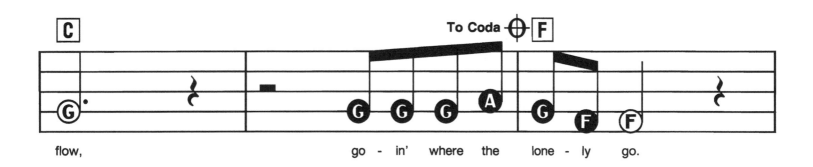

flow, go - in' where the lone - ly go.

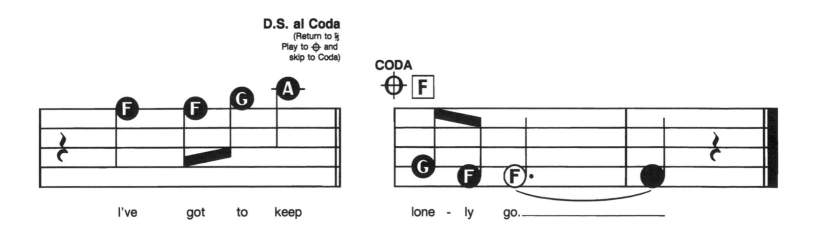

I've got to keep

lone - ly go._____

# The Fightin' Side Of Me

Registration 4
Rhythm: March or Polka

Words and Music by
Merle Haggard

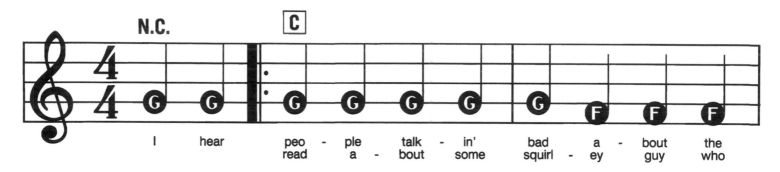

I hear peo - ple talk - in' bad a - bout the
read a - bout some squirl - ey guy who

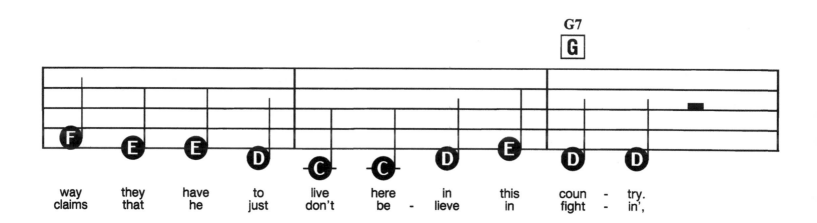

way they have to live here in this coun - try.
claims that he just don't be - lieve in fight - in',

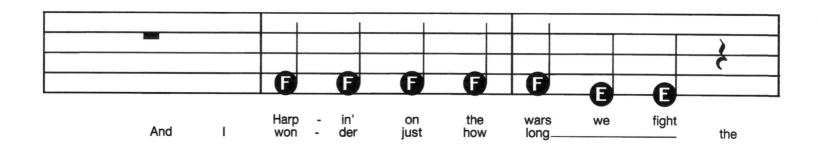

And I Harp - in' on the wars we fight the
won - der just how long

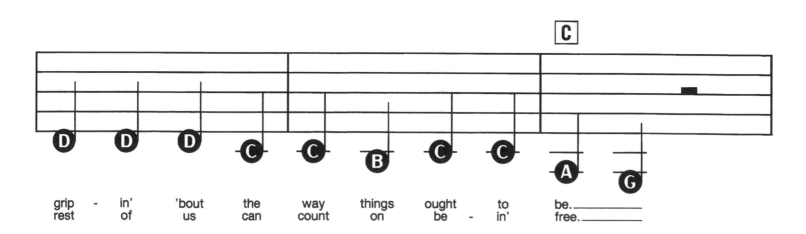

grip - in' 'bout the way things ought to be.
rest of us can count on be - in' free.

29

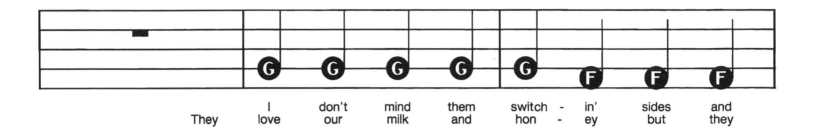

They I don't mind them switch - in' sides and
love our milk and hon - ey but they

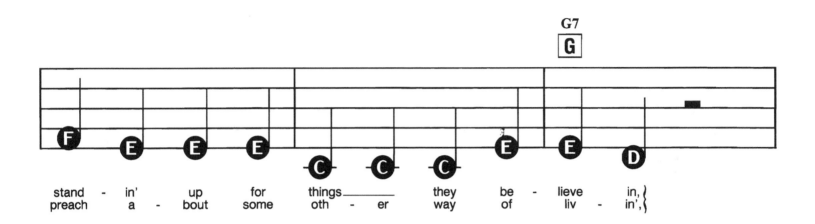

G7

stand - in' up for things____ they be - lieve in,⎰
preach a - bout some oth - er way of liv - in',⎱

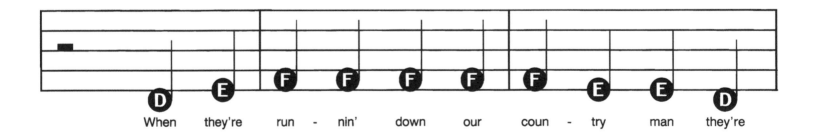

When they're run - nin' down our coun - try man they're

C

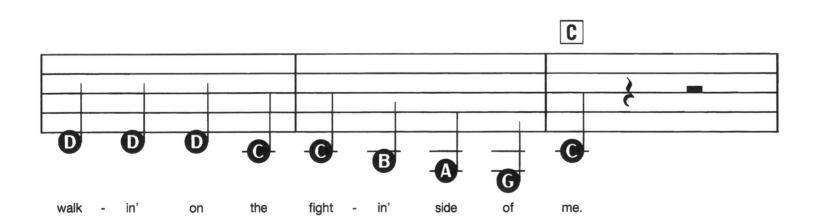

walk - in' on the fight - in' side of me.

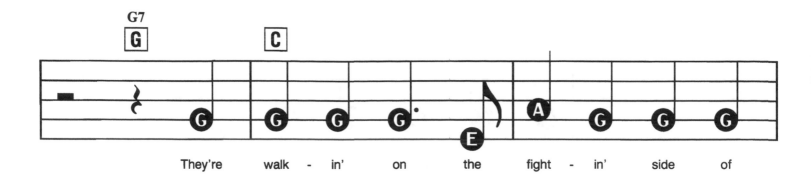

They're walk - in' on the fight - in' side of

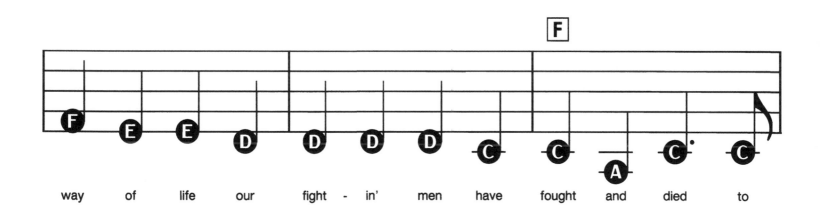

me._____ Run - nin' down a

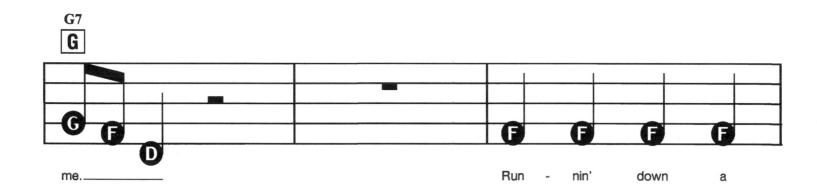

way of life our fight - in' men have fought and died to

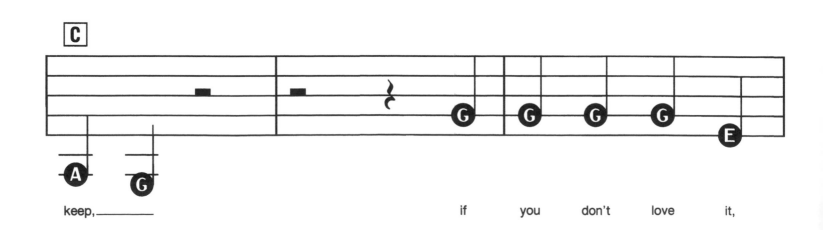

keep,_____ if you don't love it,

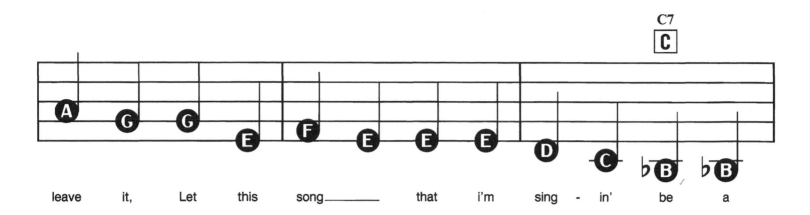

leave it, Let this song_____ that i'm sing - in' be a

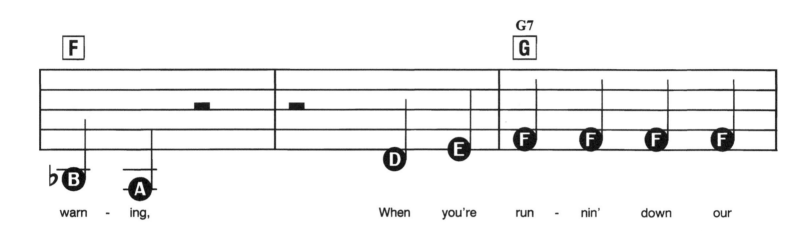

warn - ing, When you're run - nin' down our

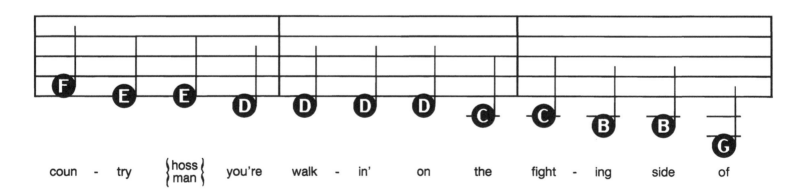

coun - try {hoss man} you're walk - in' on the fight - ing side of

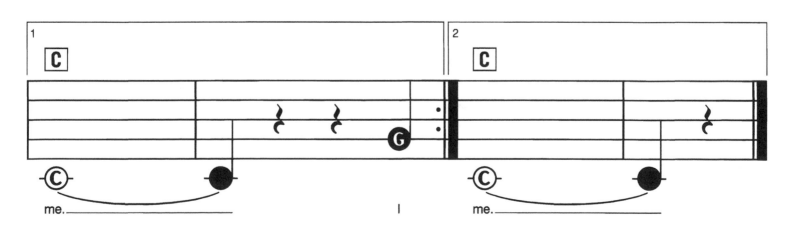

me._____ I me._____

# From Graceland To The Promised Land

Registration 4
Rhythm: Country or Shuffle

Words and Music by
Merle Haggard

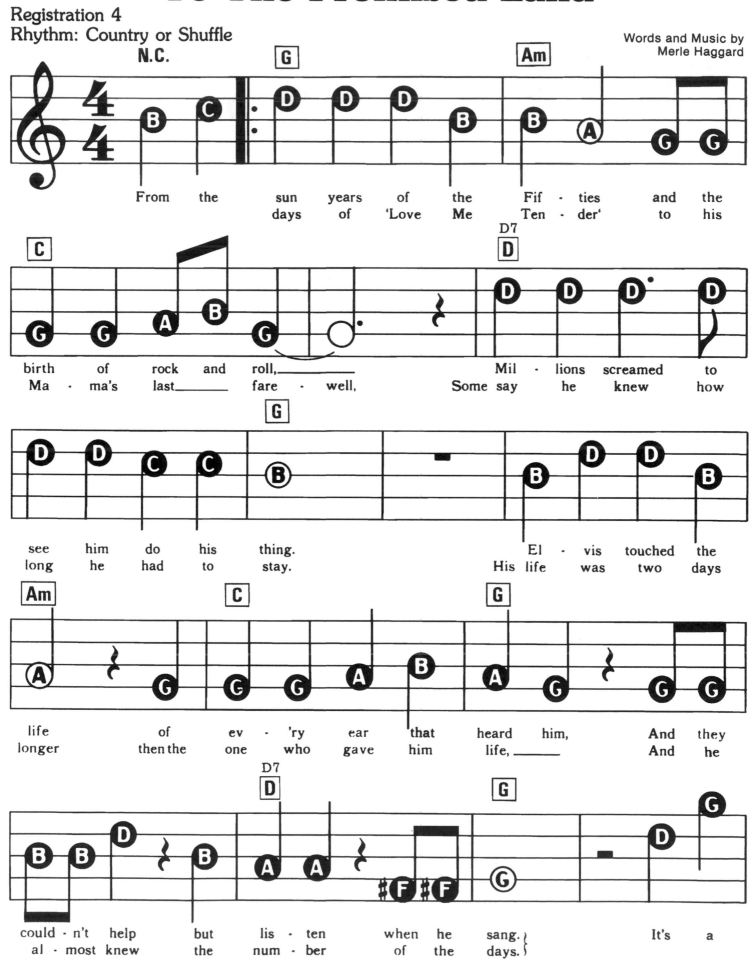

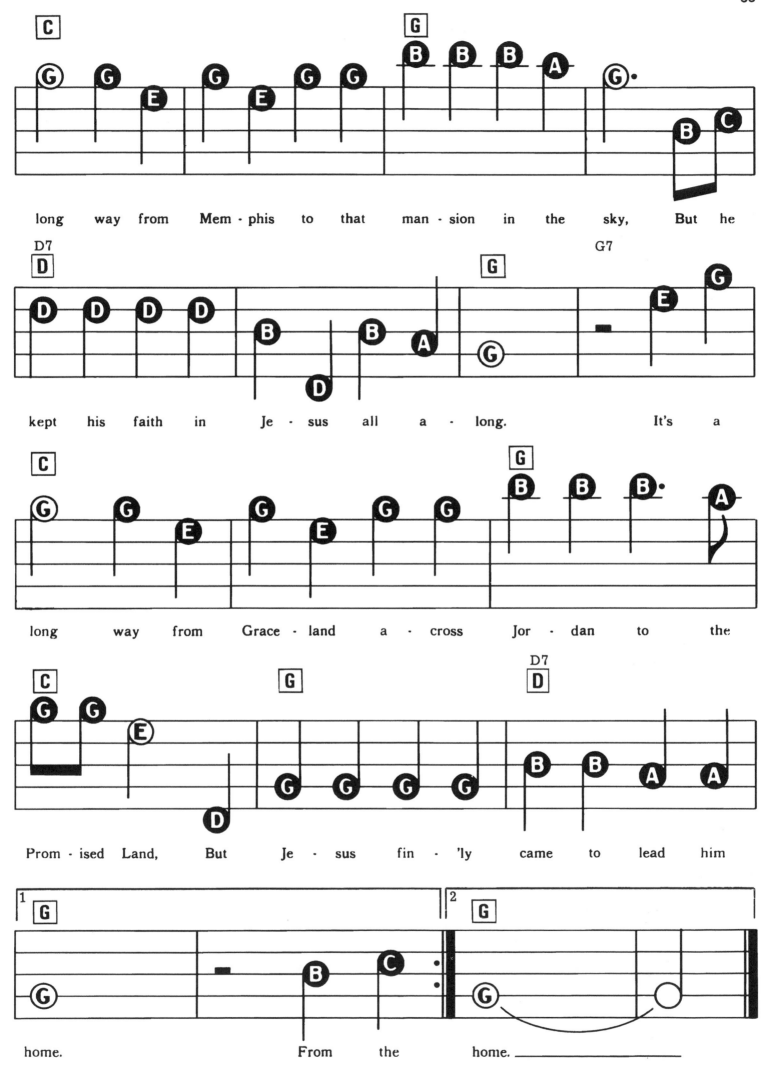

C G D7 D G G7 C G C G D7 D G G
long way from Mem - phis to that man - sion in the sky, But he
kept his faith in Je - sus all a - long. It's a
long way from Grace - land a - cross Jor - dan to the
Prom - ised Land, But Je - sus fin - 'ly came to lead him
1 home. From the
2 home.

# Grandma Harp

Registration 8
Rhythm: Country or March

Words and Music by
Merle Haggard

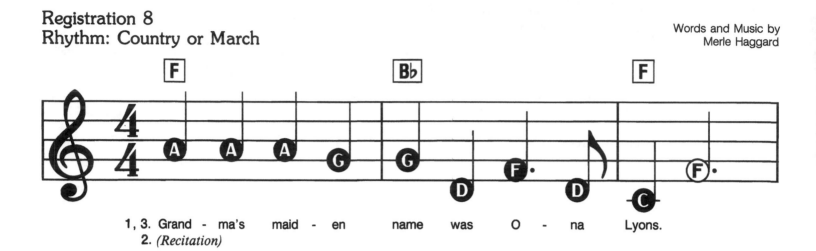

1, 3. Grand - ma's maid - en name was O - na Lyons.
2. *(Recitation)*

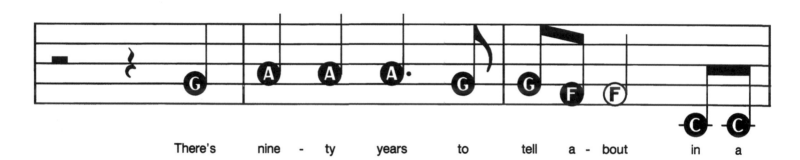

There's nine - ty years to tell a - bout in a

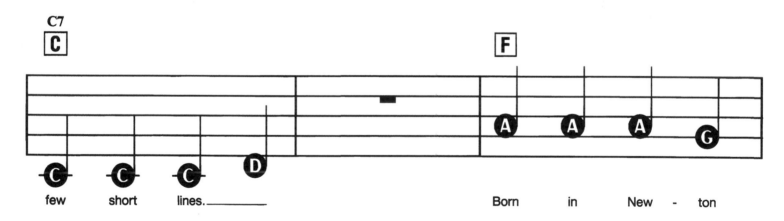

few short lines._____ Born in New - ton

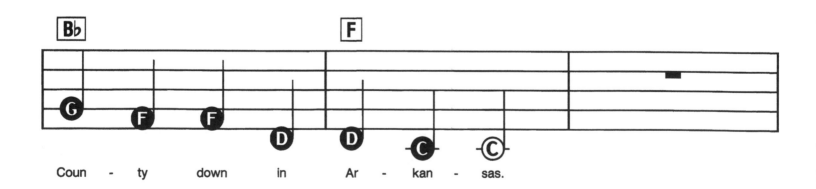

Coun - ty down in Ar - kan - sas.

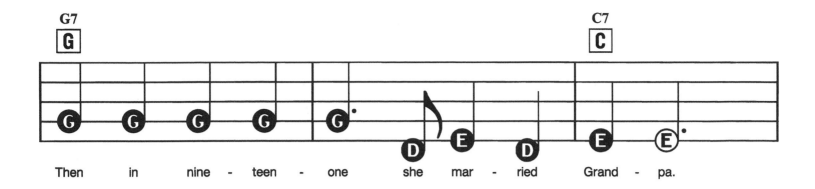

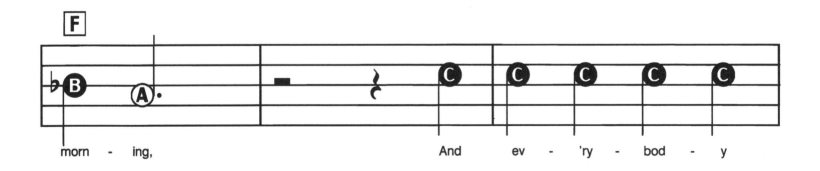

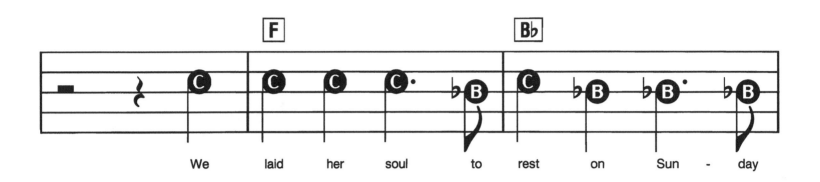

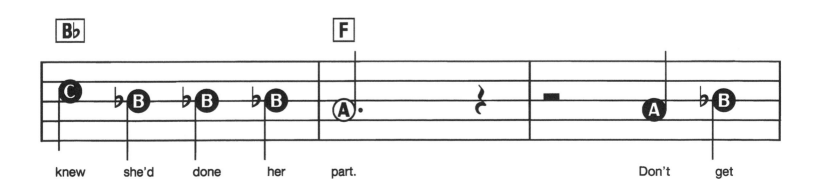

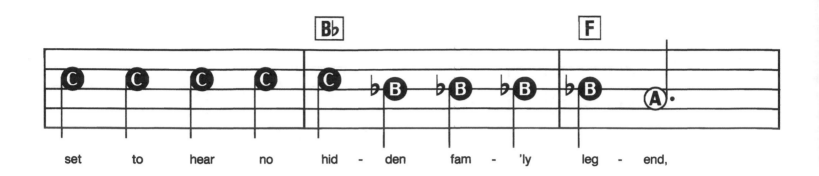

set       to       hear       no       hid - den     fam - 'ly     leg - end,

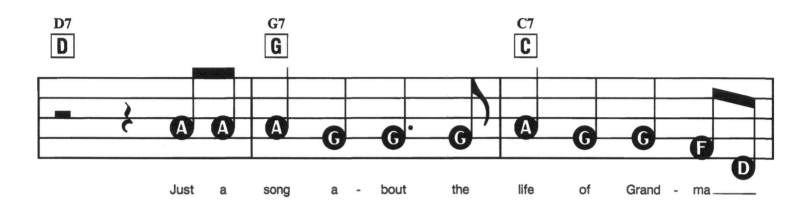

Just     a     song     a - bout     the     life     of     Grand - ma_____

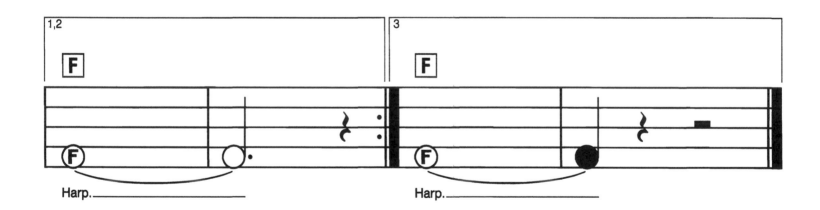

Harp._____              Harp._____

*Recitation*

2. *Just think about the times that she lived through,*
*And think about the changin' world she saw.*
*Now, somehow she reared a decent family out of poverty,*
*And for seventy years she loved the same old Grandpa.*
*To me her passing brought a closin' chapter*
*To a way of life that I loved within my heart.*
*I just mean to say I think we owe her somethin' special,*
*(Sung)* If just a song about the life of Grandma Harp.

# I Take A Lot Of Pride In What I Am

Registration 10
Rhythm: Rock or March

Words and Music by
Merle Haggard

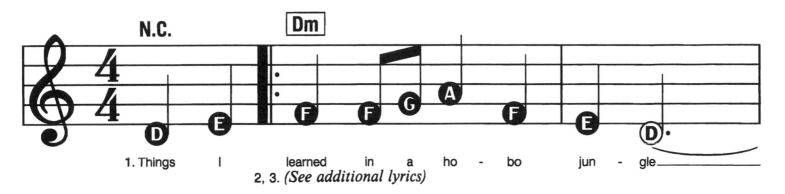

1. Things I learned in a ho-bo jun-gle
2, 3. *(See additional lyrics)*

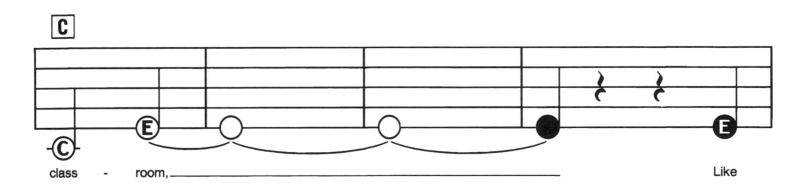

were things they nev - er taught me in a

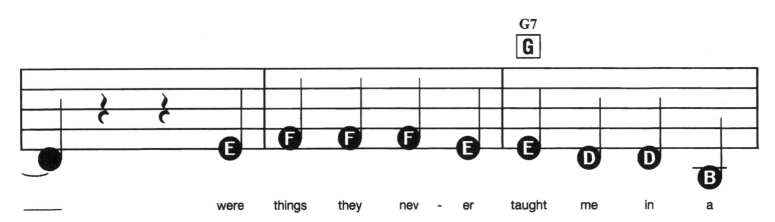

class - room,_____ Like

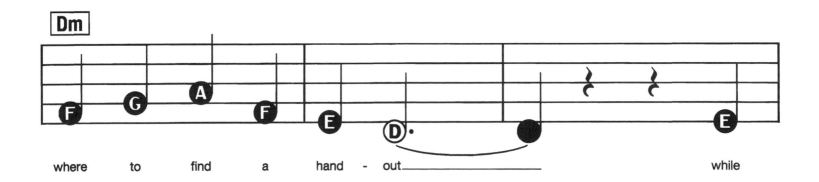

where to find a hand - out_____ while

38

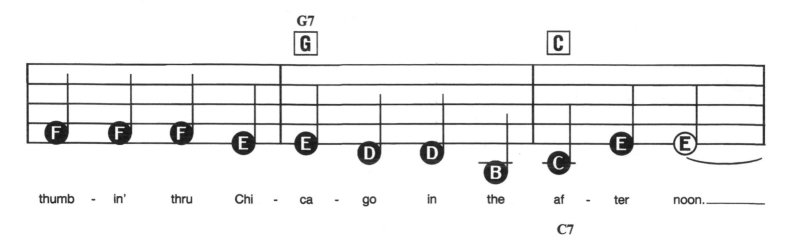

thumb - in' thru Chi - ca - go in the af - ter noon._____

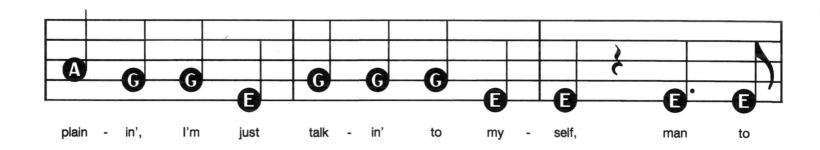

Hey, I'm not brag - gin' or com -

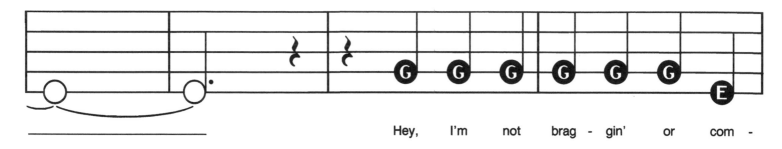

plain - in', I'm just talk - in' to my - self, man to

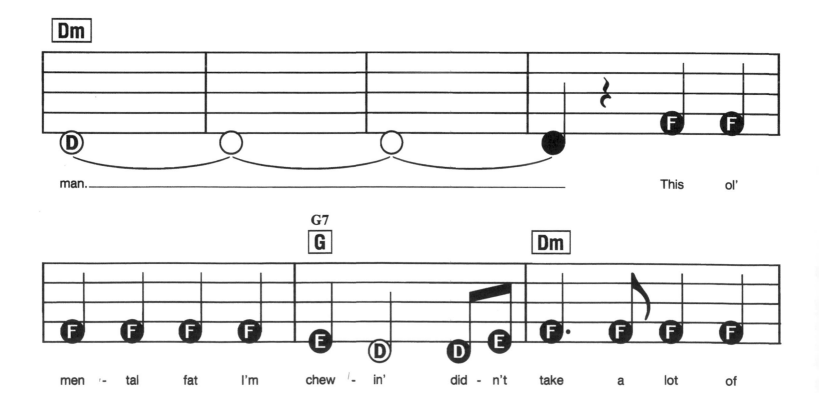

man._____ This ol'

men - tal fat I'm chew - in' did - n't take a lot of

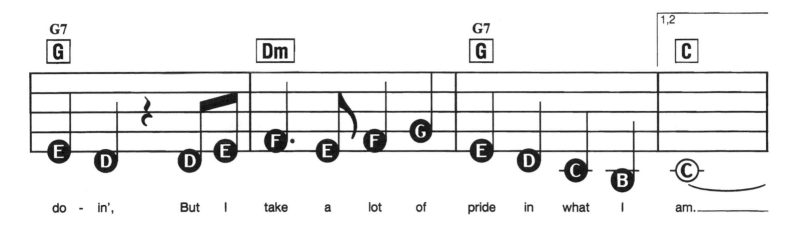

do - in', But I take a lot of pride in what I am.

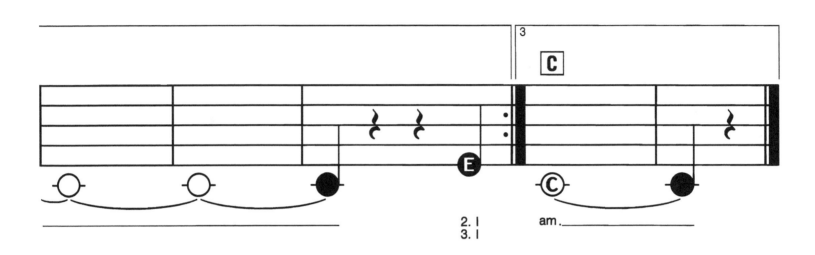

2. I
3. I

am.

Additional Lyrics

2. I guess I grew up a loner, I don't remember ever havin' any folks around,
   But I keep thumbin' thru the phone books, And lookin' for my daddy's name in every town.
   And I meet lots of friendly people, that I always end up leavin' on the lam.
   Hey, where I've been or where I'm goin' didn't take a lot of knowin',
   But I take a lot of pride in what I am.

3. I never travel in a hurry, 'Cause I got nobody waitin' for me anywhere.
   Home is anywhere I'm livin', If it's sleepin' on some vacant bench in City Square,
   Or if I'm workin' on some road gang, or just livin' off the fat of our great land.
   I never been nobody's idol, But at least I got a title,
   And I take a lot of pride in what I am.

# Hungry Eyes

Registration 9
Rhythm: Country or Rock

Words and Music by
Merle Haggard

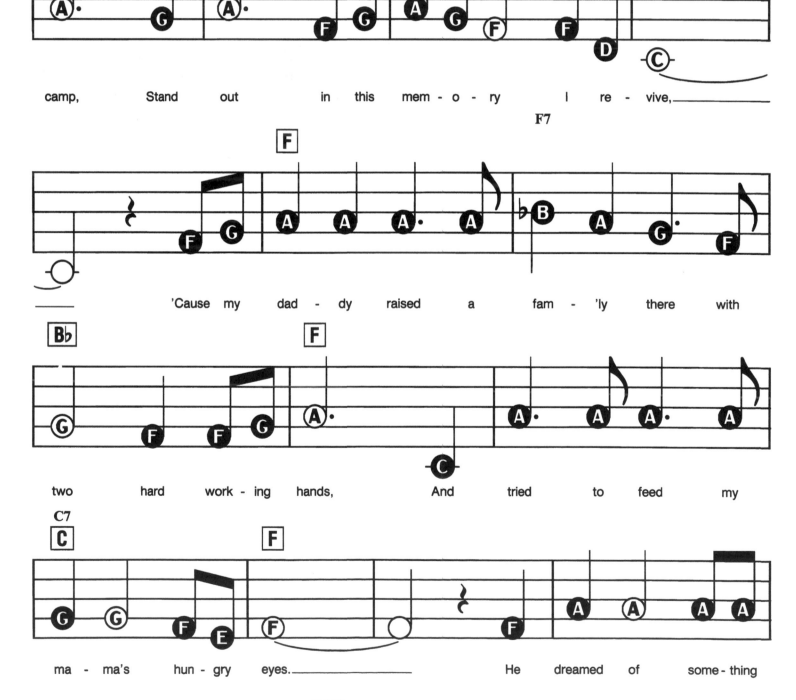

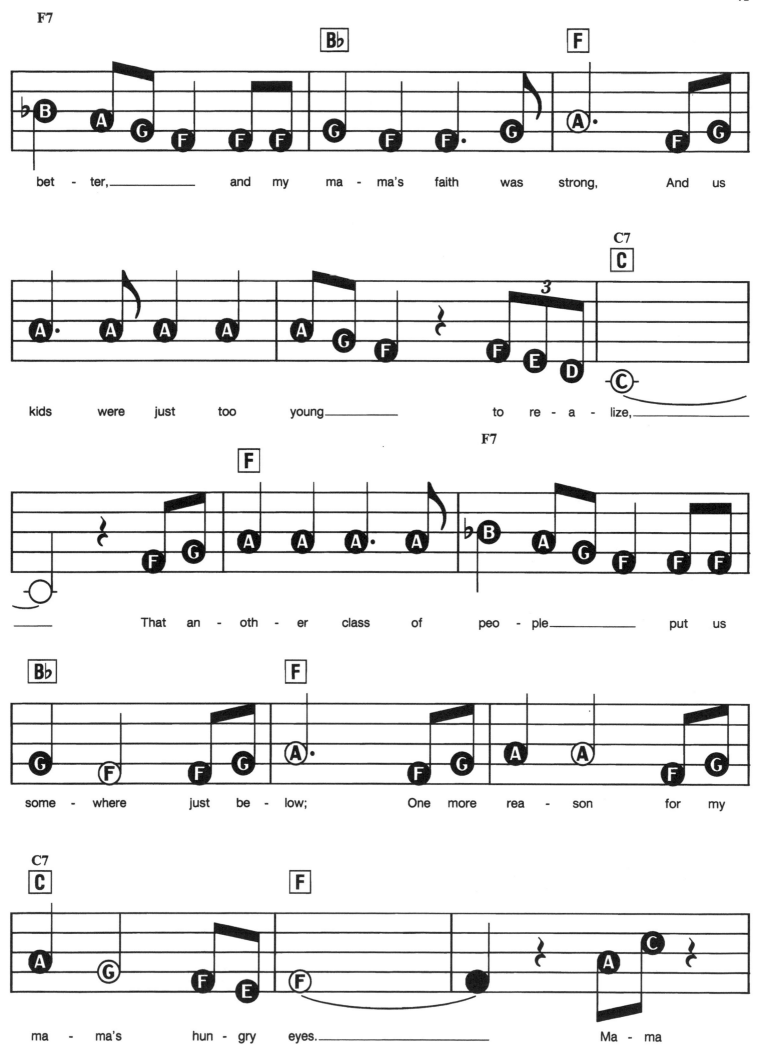

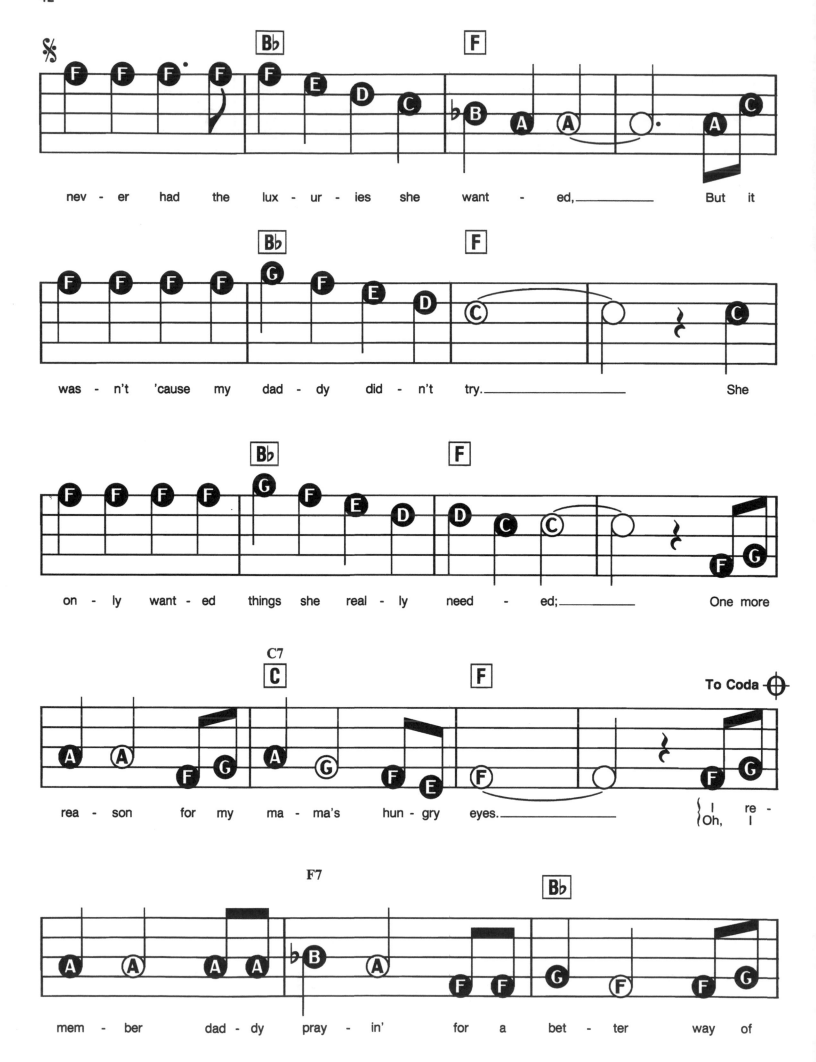

life, But I don't re - call a change of an - y size. Just a lit - tle loss of cour - age as their age_____ be - gan to show, And more sad - ness in my ma - ma's hun - gry eyes._____ Ma - ma still re - call my ma - ma's hun - gry eyes._____

# I Had A Beautiful Time

Registration 10
Rhythm: Country or March

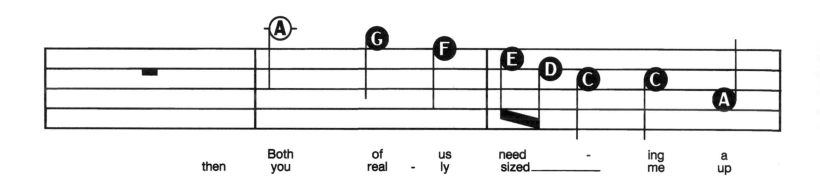

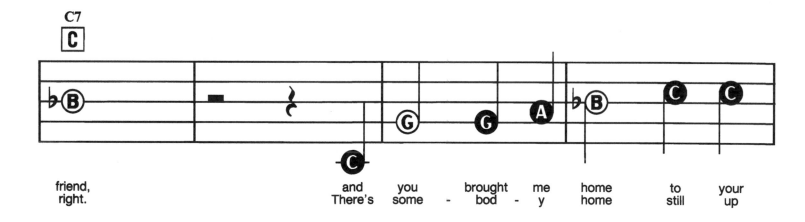

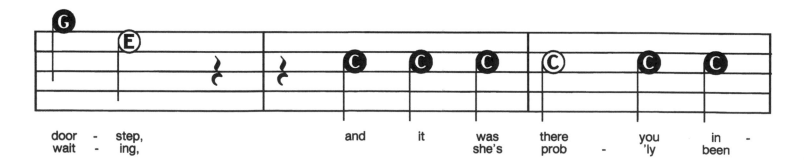

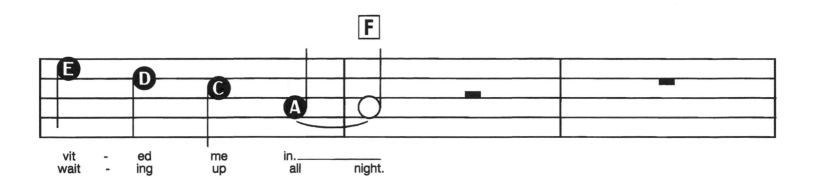

vit - ed me in._____
wait - ing up all night.

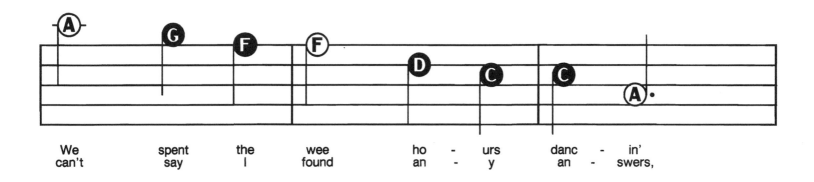

We spent the wee ho - urs danc - in'
can't say I found an - y an - swers,

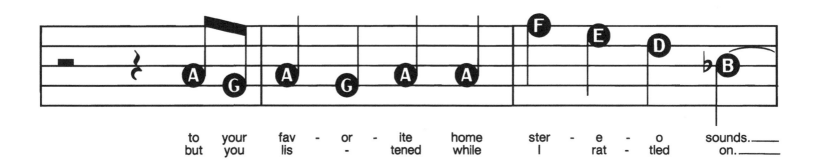

to your fav - or - ite home ster - e - o sounds.____
but you lis - tened while I rat - tled on.____

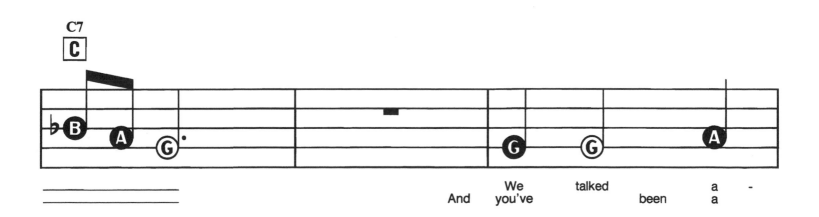

_____
_____

We talked been a -
And you've been a

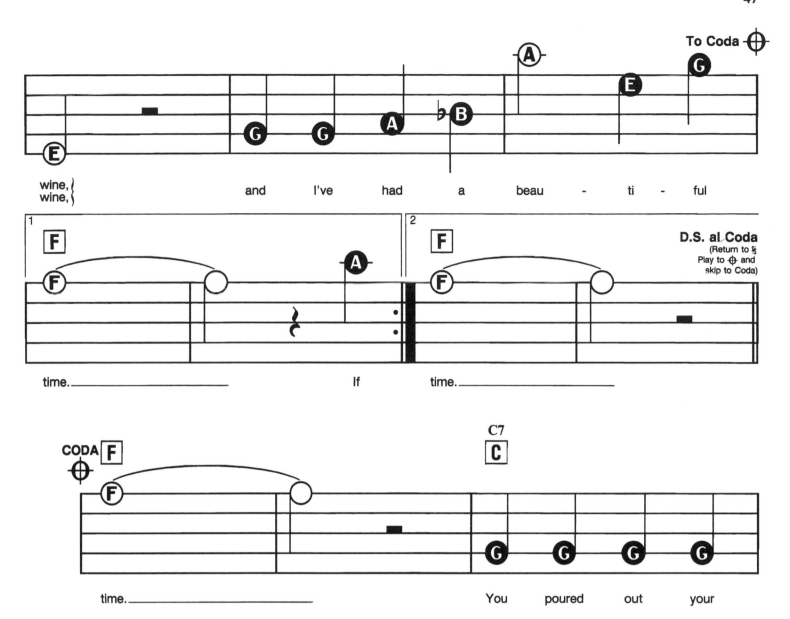

wine, / wine, ꞵ and I've had a beau - ti - ful

**1** **F**  **2** **F**  **D.S. al Coda**
(Return to 𝄋
Play to ⊕ and
skip to Coda)

time._____ If time._____

**CODA** **F**  **C7** **C**

time._____ You poured out your

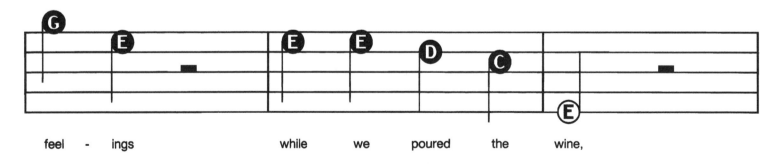

feel - ings while we poured the wine,

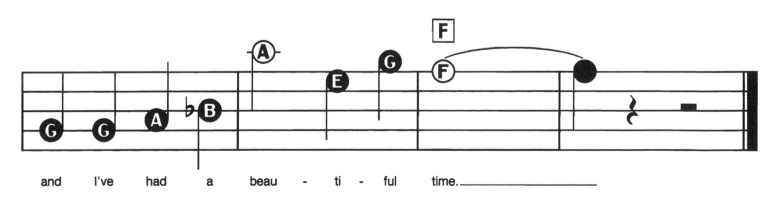

and I've had a beau - ti - ful time._____

# I Think I'll Just Stay Here And Drink

Registration 9
Rhythm: Ballad

Words and Music by
Merle Haggard

Could be hold-ing you to - night
hear that loud juke - box play-in'

could quit do - ing wrong, start

do - ing right._____
in my ear._____

You don't care a - bout what I think,
Ain't no wom - an gon' change the way I think,

think I'll just stay here and_____ drink.
think I'll just stay here and_____ drink.

Hey, put - ting you down won't square the deal,
Hey, hurt - ing me now don't mean a thing,

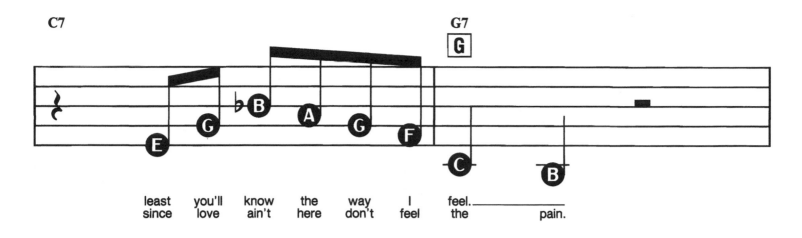

least you'll know the way I feel. ___
since love ain't here don't feel the pain.

Hey, take all the mon - ey in the bank.
My mind ain't nothing but a to - tal blank.

Think I'll just stay here and ___ drink.
Think I'll just stay here and ___

Hey, lis - ten close and you can

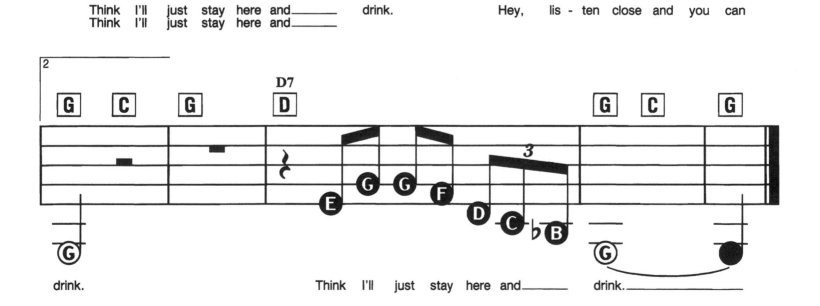

drink.

Think I'll just stay here and ___ drink. ___

# I Threw Away The Rose

Registration 1
Rhythm: Country or Rock

Words and Music by
Merle Haggard

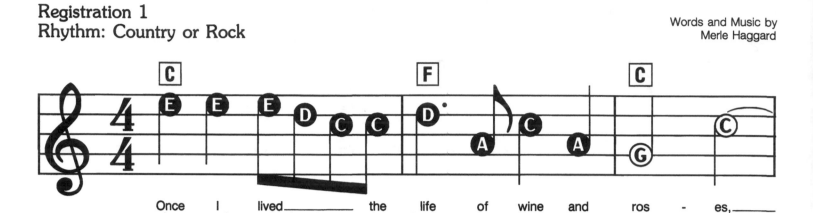

Once I lived_____ the life of wine and ros - es,_____
by and watched the bottle take con - trol of me,_____

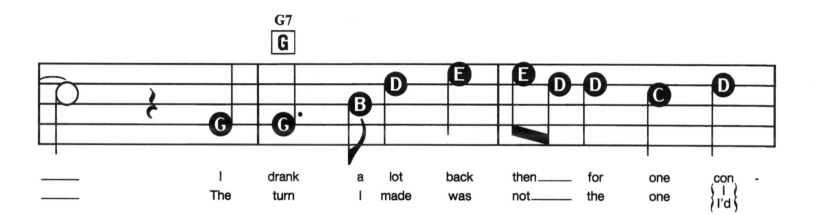

_____ I drank a lot back then_____ for one con -
The turn I made was not_____ the one {I / I'd}

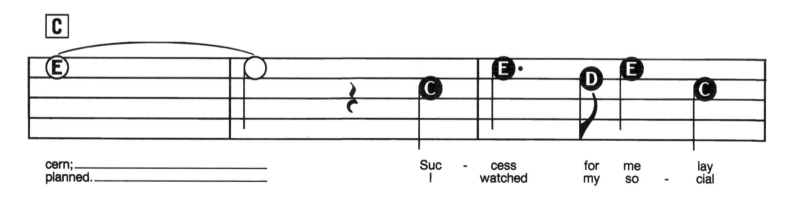

cern;_____
planned._____ Suc - cess for me lay
I watched my so - cial

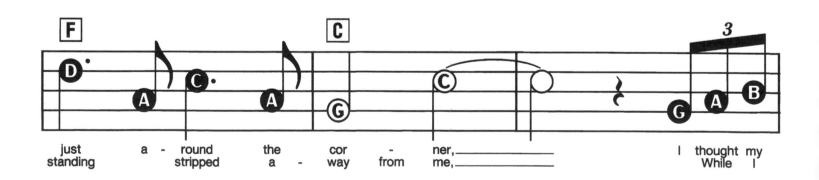

just a - round the cor - ner,_____ I thought my
standing stripped a - way from me,_____ While I

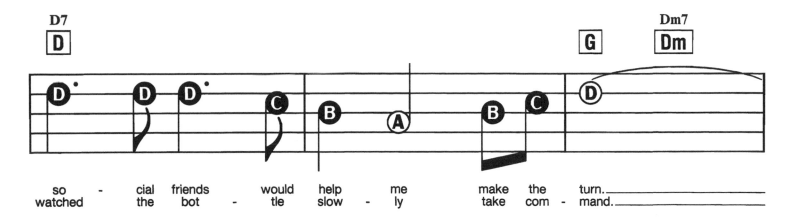

so - cial friends would help me make the turn._____
watched the bot - tle slow - ly take com - mand._____

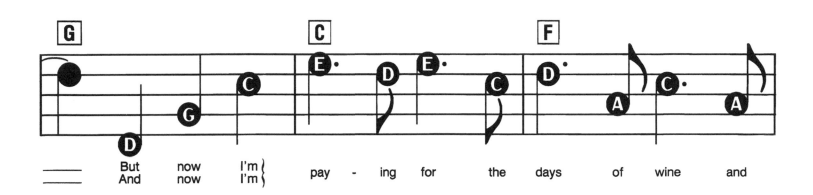

_____ But now I'm { pay - ing for the days of wine and
_____ And now I'm {

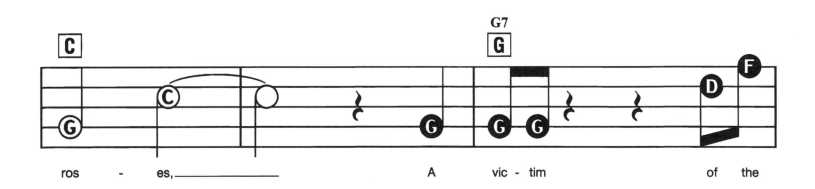

ros - es,_____ A vic - tim of the

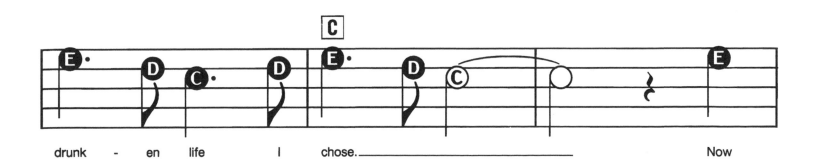

drunk - en life I chose._____ Now

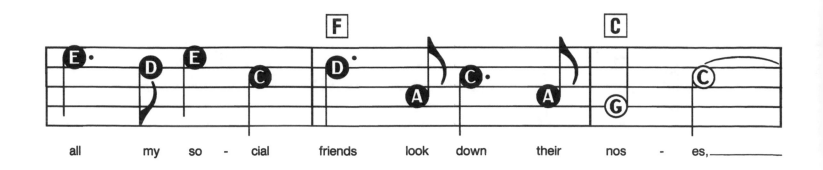

all my so - cial friends look down their nos - es,

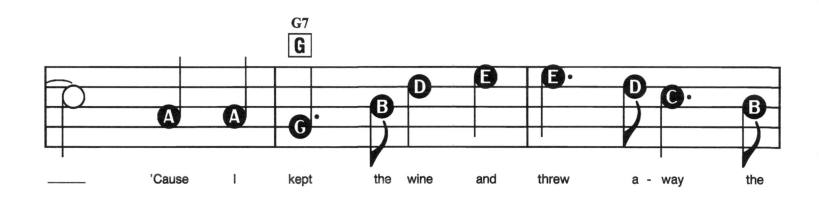

'Cause I kept the wine and threw a - way the

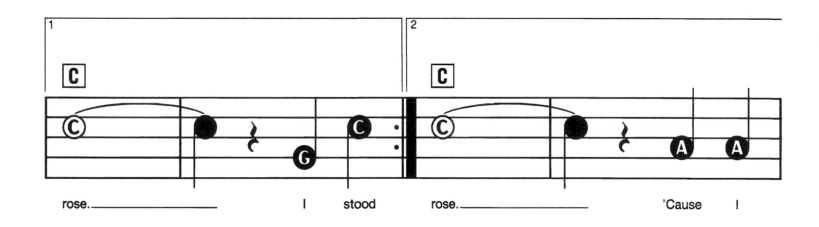

rose. I stood rose. 'Cause I

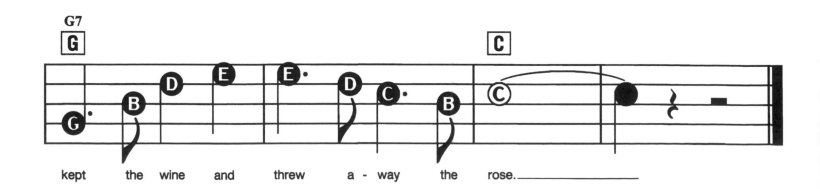

kept the wine and threw a - way the rose.

# If We Make It Through December

Registration 4
Rhythm: Country or Shuffle

Words and Music by
Merle Haggard

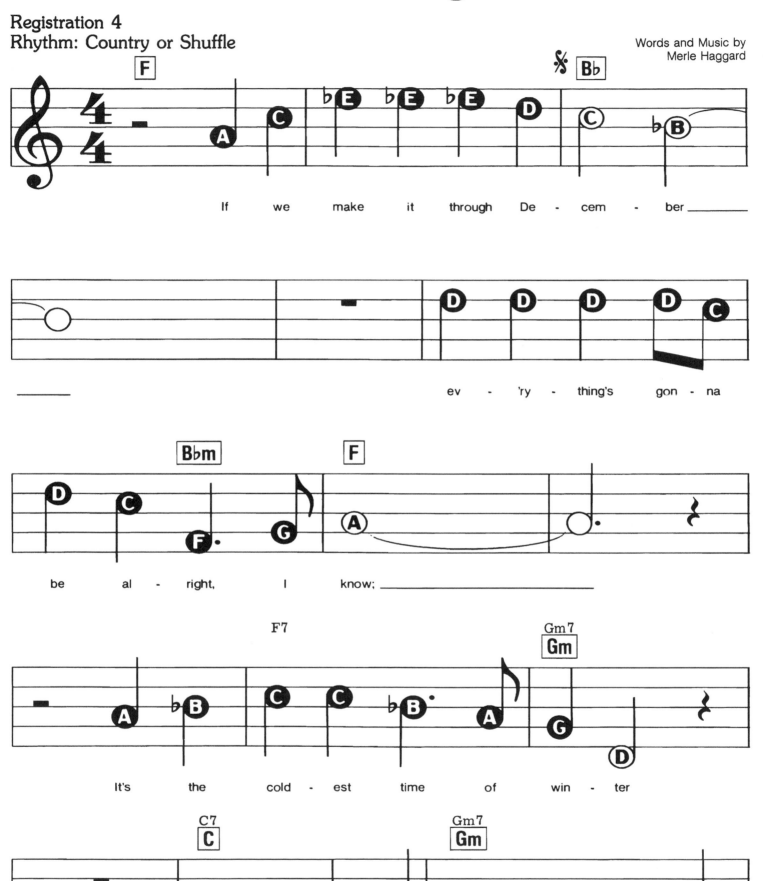

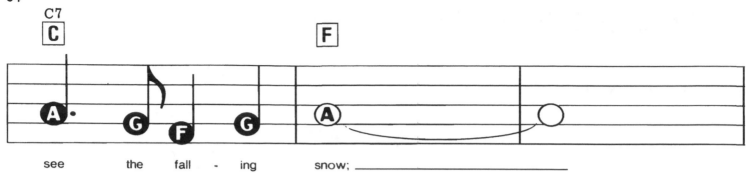

see the fall - ing snow; _____

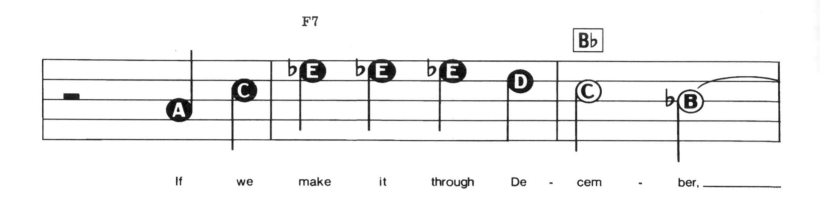

If we make it through De - cem - ber, _____

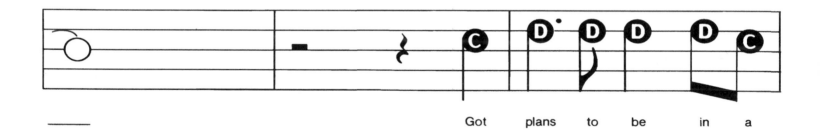

_____ Got plans to be in a

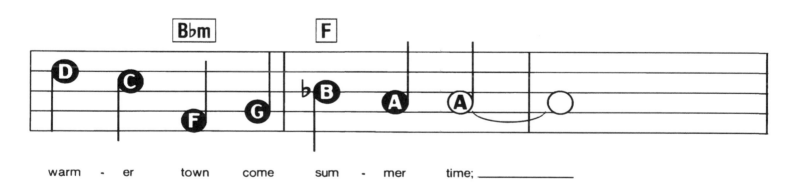

warm - er town come sum - mer time; _____

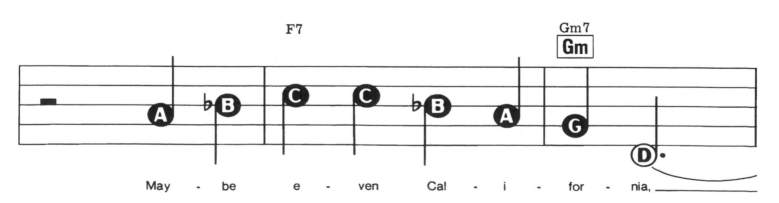

May - be e - ven Cal - i - for - nia, _____

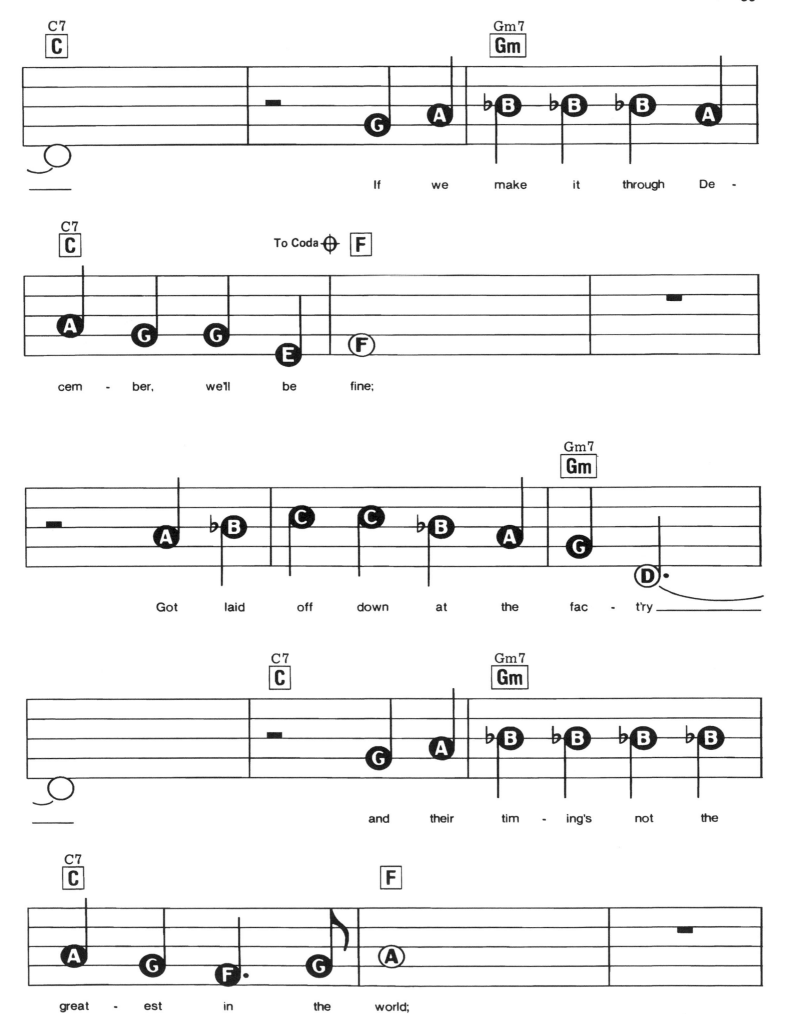

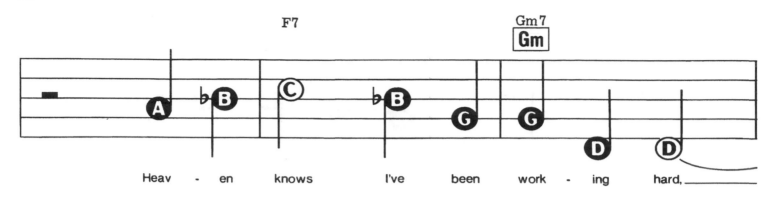

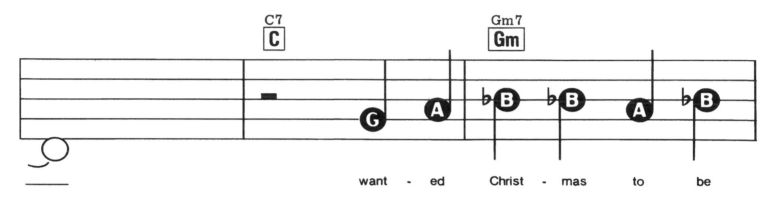

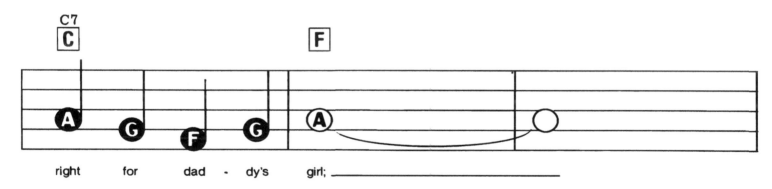

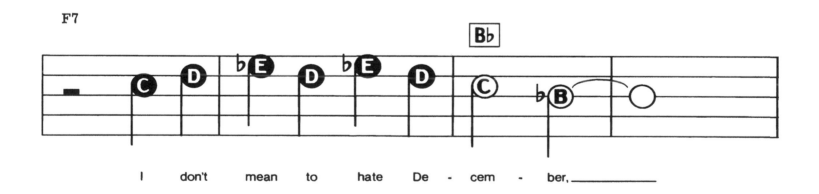

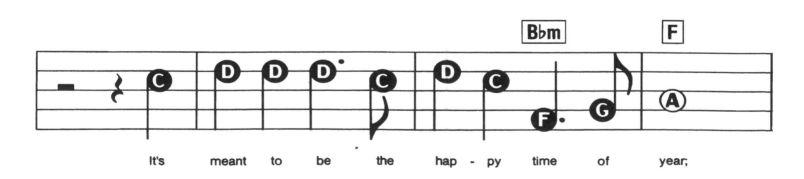

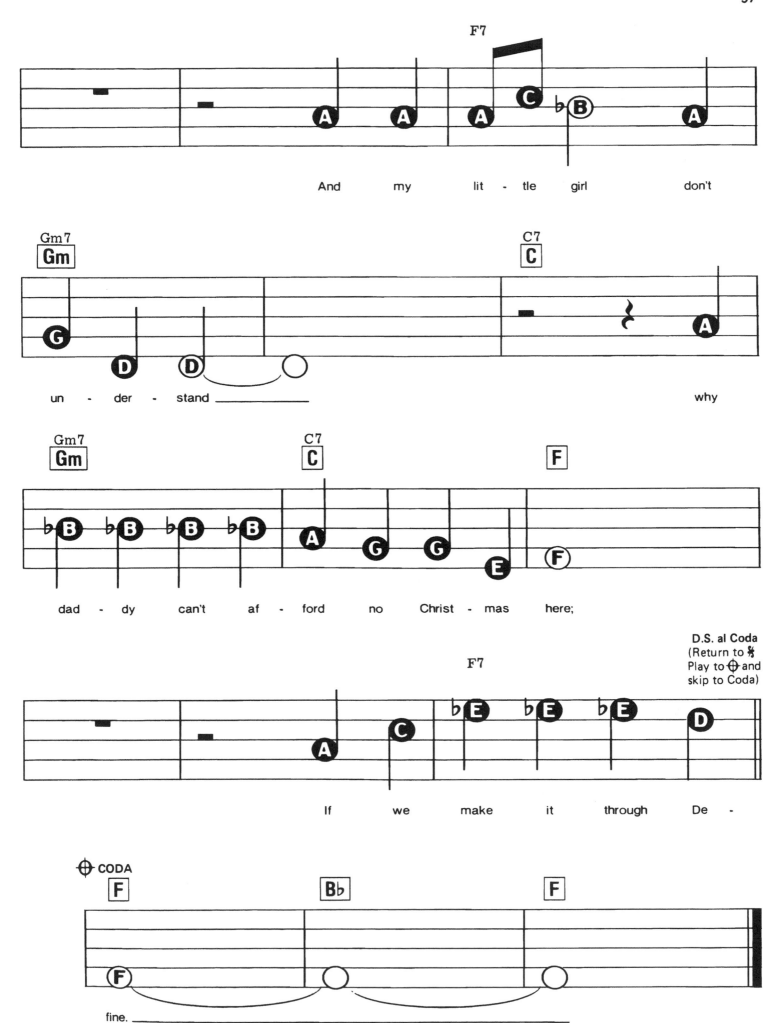

# I Wonder If They Ever Think Of Me

Registration 8
Rhythm: March or Country

Words and Music by
Merle Haggard

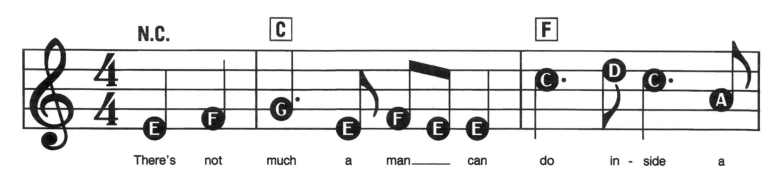

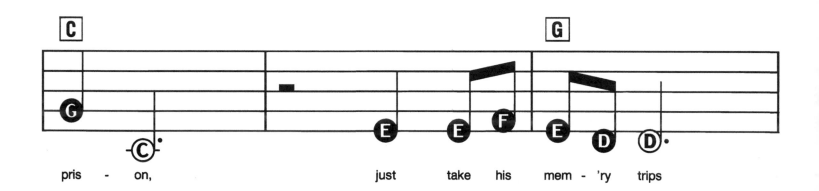

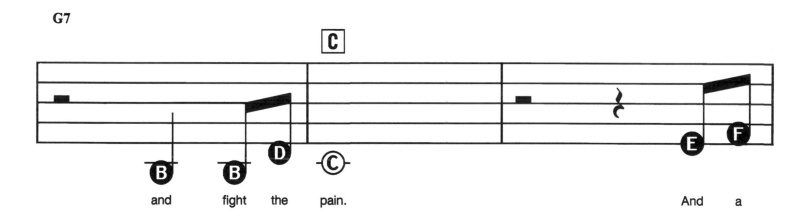

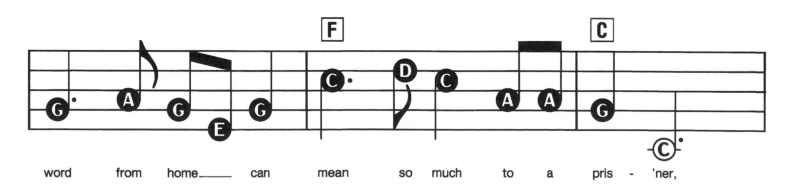

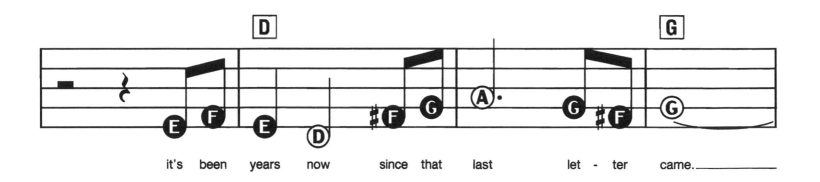

it's been years now since that last let - ter came.____

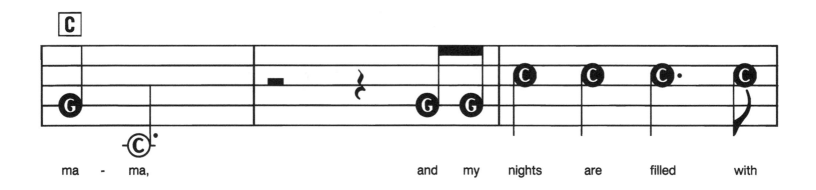

____ Not a day goes by____ that I don't think of

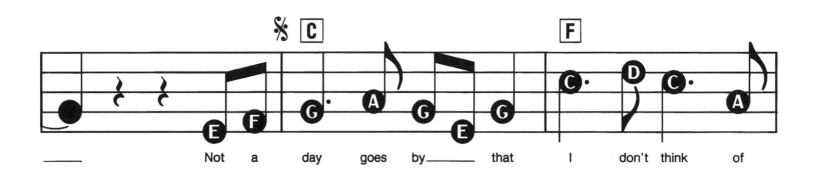

ma - ma, and my nights are filled with

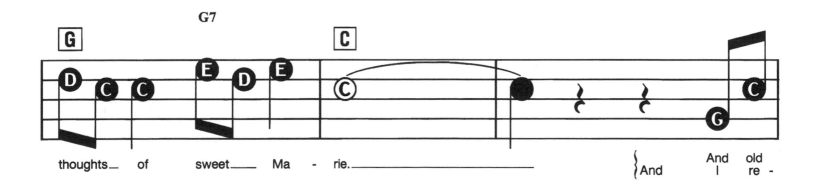

thoughts__ of sweet__ Ma - rie.____ {And And old I re -

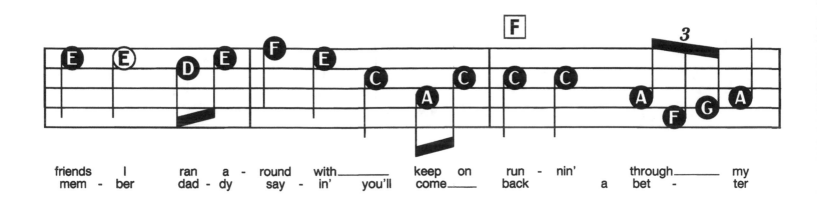

friends I ran a - round with_____ keep on run - nin' through_____ my
mem - ber dad - dy say - in' you'll come_____ back a bet - ter

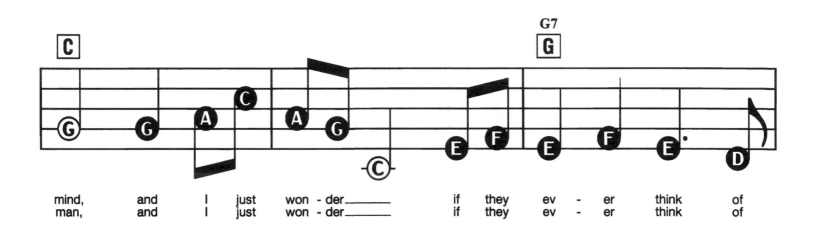

mind, and I just won - der_____ if they ev - er think of
man, and I just won - der_____ if they ev - er think of

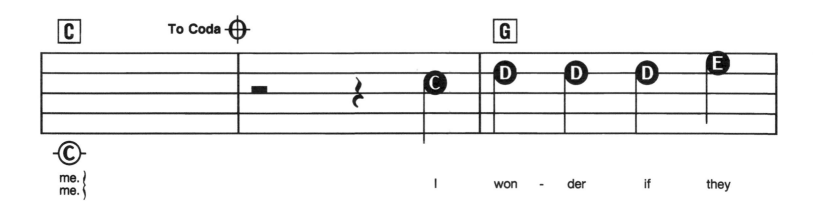

me.
me.
I won - der if they

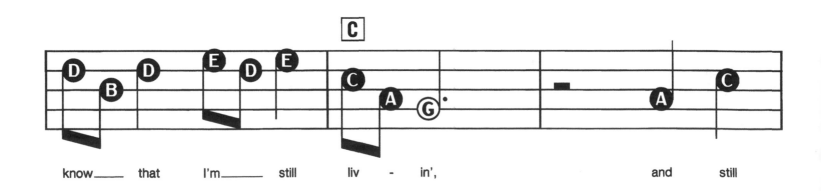

know_____ that I'm_____ still liv - in', and still

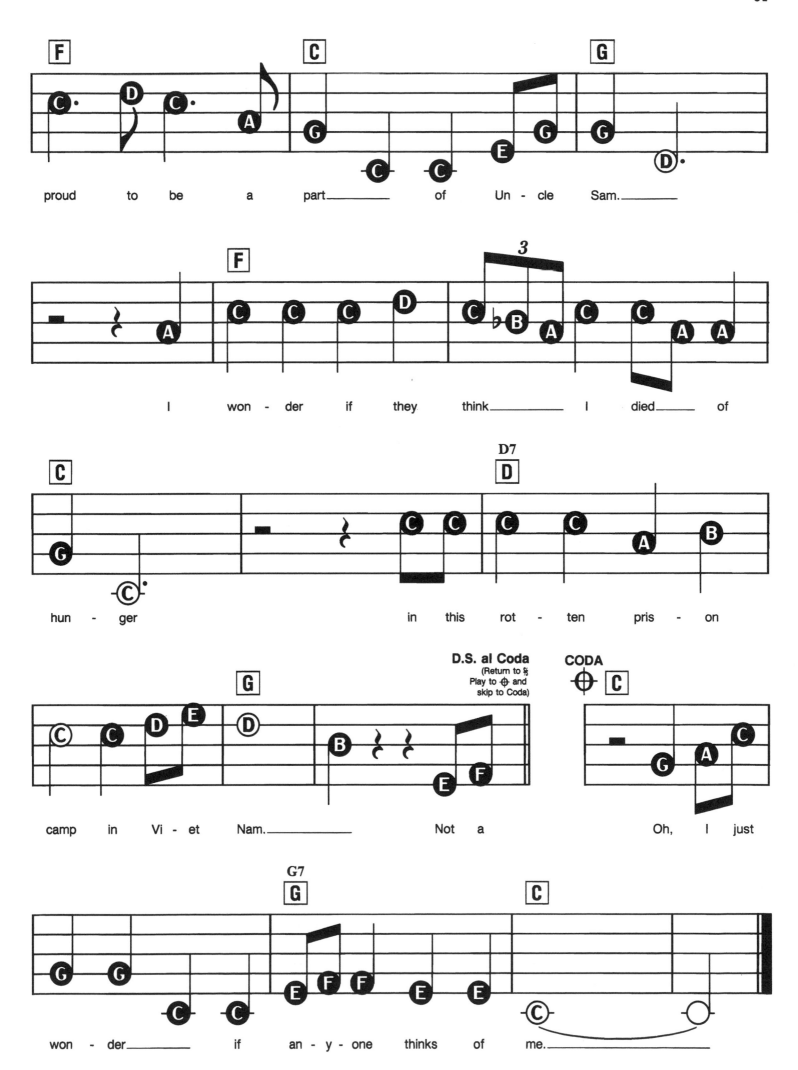

# I'm Always On A Mountain When I Fall

Registration 8
Rhythm: Country or Rock

Words and Music by
Merle Haggard

**G**

Most of my life I've al - most been a win - ner.
Then you came along and had me be - liev - in'

**Am**

**D7**
**D**

I've come so close but nev - er real - ly
for once in my life my luck_____ fi - n'lly

**G**

won. Just when I thought I fi - n'lly
changed. And now you say you're gon - na

**C**

made it, I
leave me. Seems

**D7**
**D**

find my - self back
ev - 'ry - thing I

# It's All In The Movies

Registration 3
Rhythm: Pops or Rock

Words and Music by
Merle Haggard and Kelli Haggard

# If We're Not Back In Love By Monday

Registration 7
Rhythm: Country or Rock

Words and Music by
Sonny Throckmorton and Glenn Martin

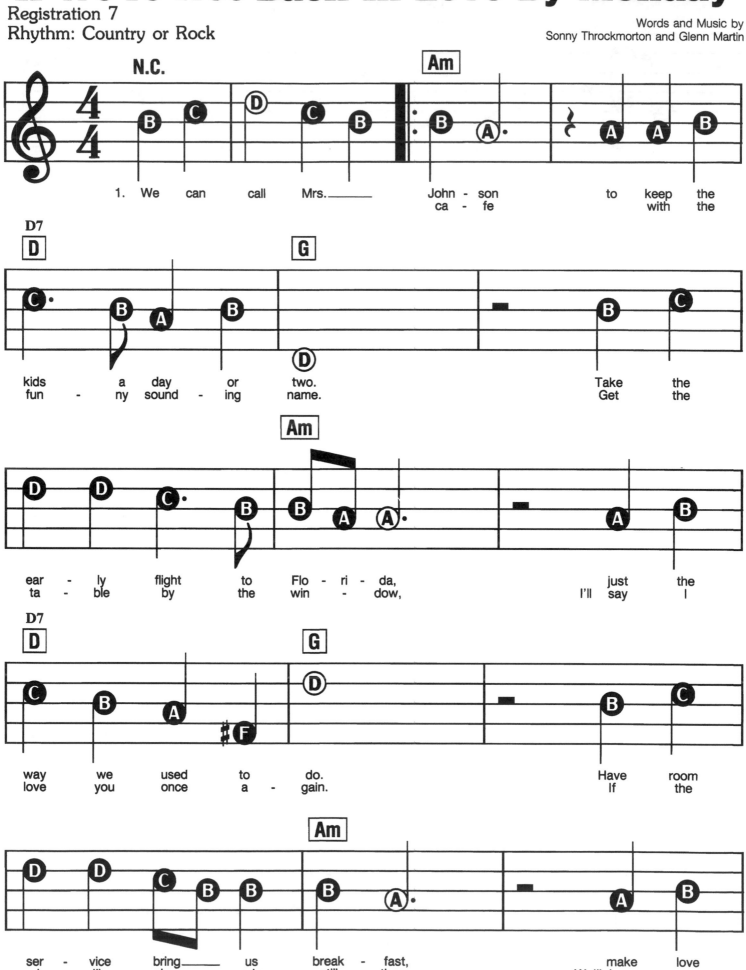

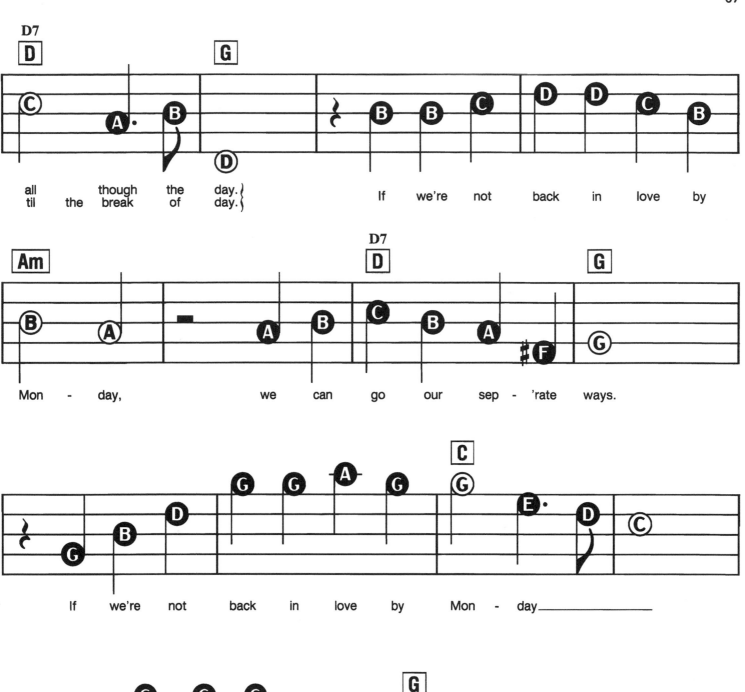

all til the though break the of day. day.  If we're not back in love by

Mon - day, we can go our sep - 'rate ways.

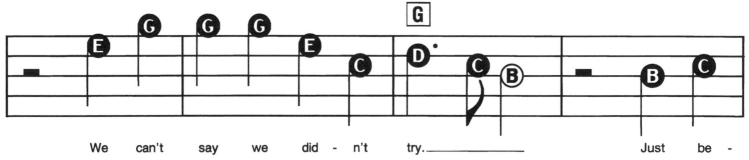

If we're not back in love by Mon - day_____

We can't say we did - n't try._____ Just be -

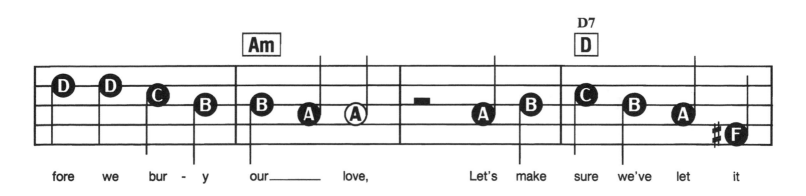

fore we bur - y our_____ love, Let's make sure we've let it

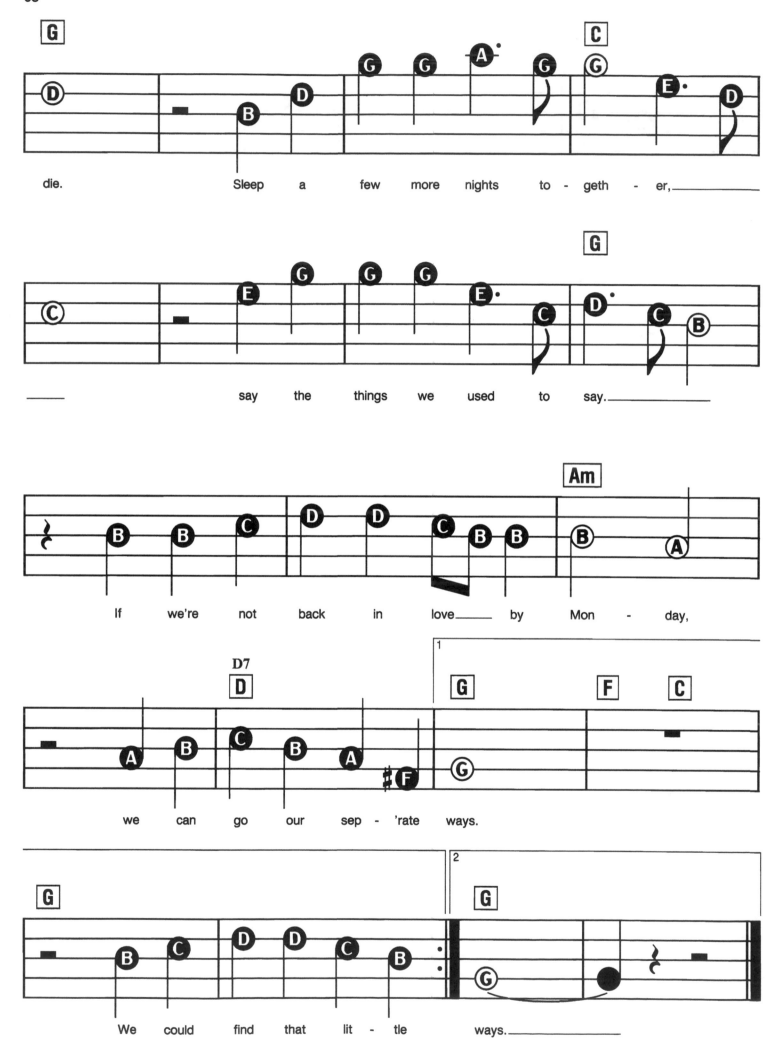

# It's Been A Great Afternoon

Registration 1
Rhythm: Country Western

Words and Music by
Merle Haggard

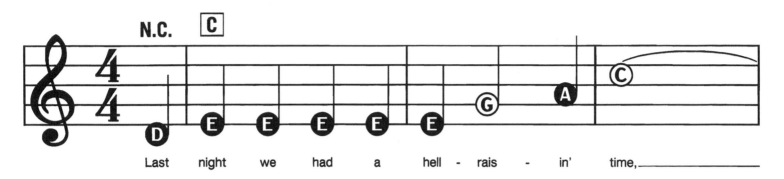

Last night we had a hell-rais-in' time,_____

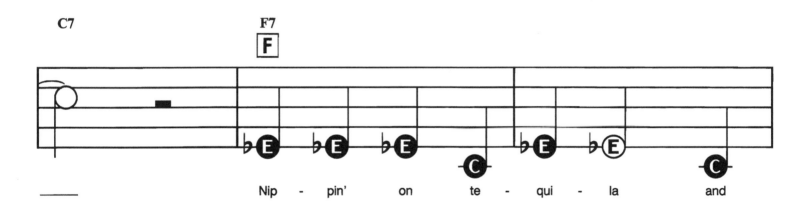

_____ Nip - pin' on te - qui - la and

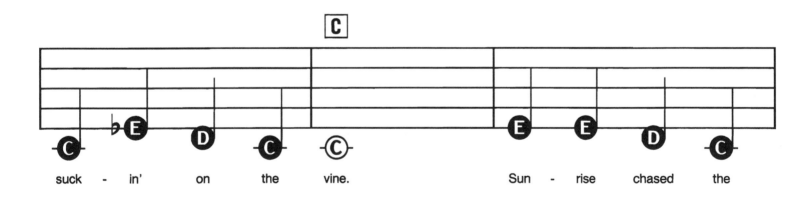

suck - in' on the vine. Sun - rise chased the

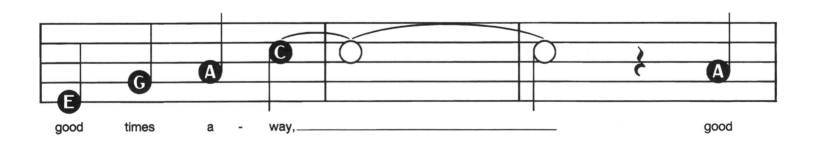

good times a - way,_____ good

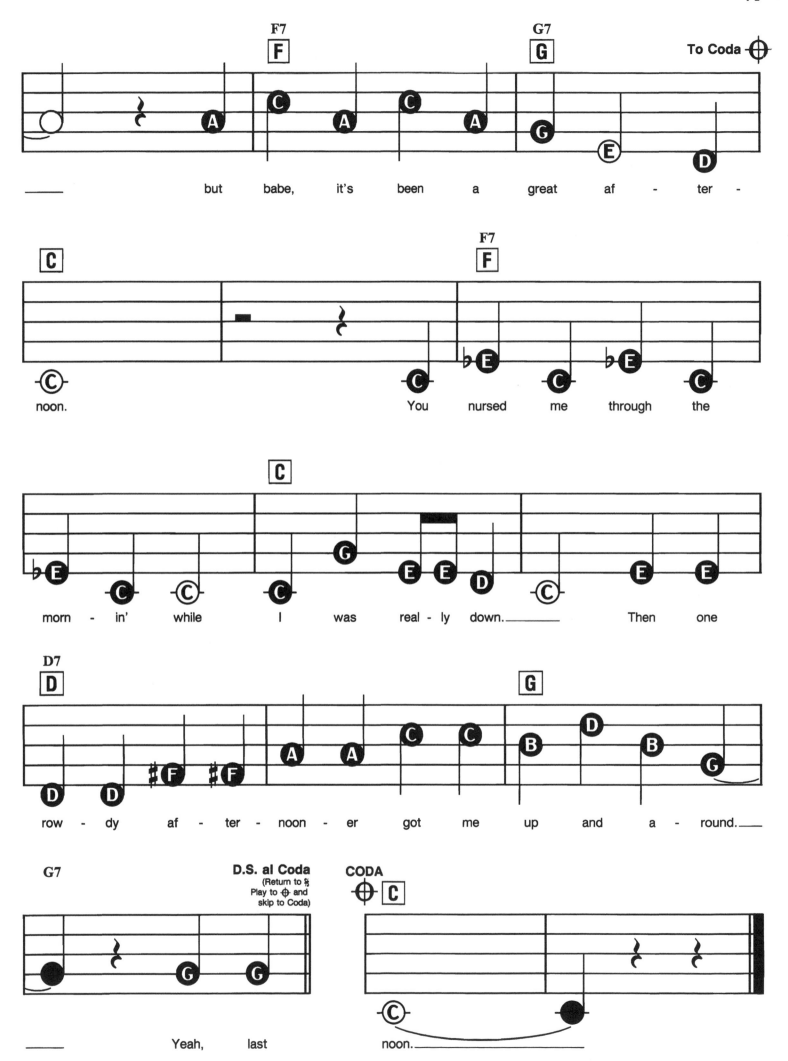

# It's Not Love
## (But It's Not Bad)

Registration 5
Rhythm: Swing or Jazz

Words and Music by
Glenn Martin and Hank Cochran

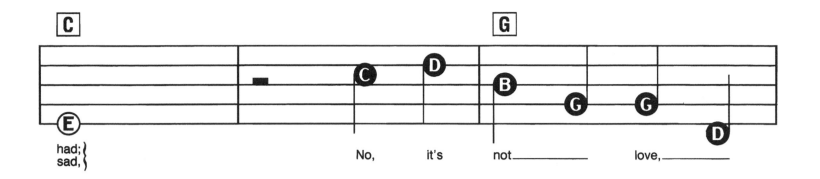

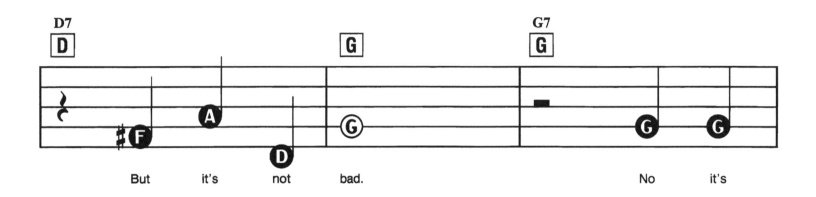

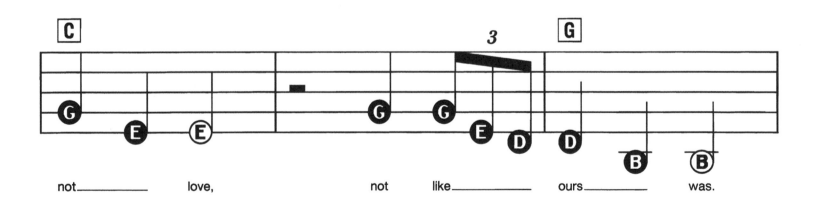

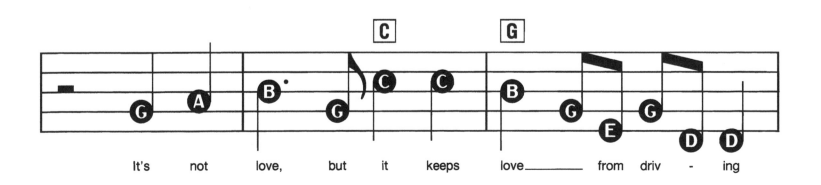

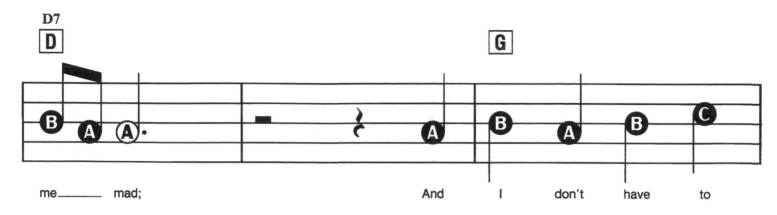

me_____ mad; And I don't have to

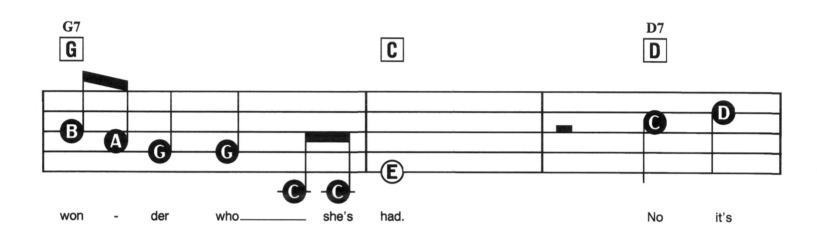

won - der who_____ she's had. No it's

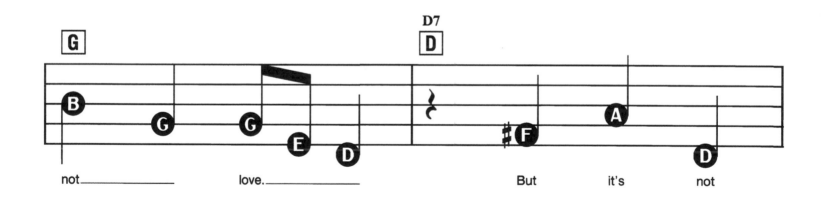

not_____ love._____ But it's not

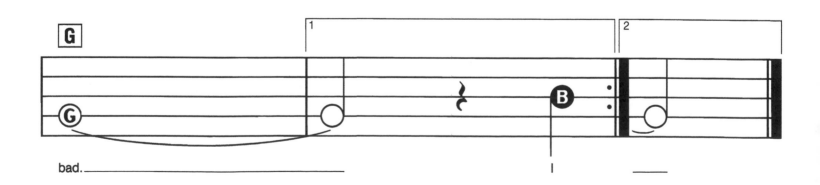

bad._____

# Jesus, Take A Hold

Registration 10
Rhythm: Country or Rock

Words and Music by
Merle Haggard

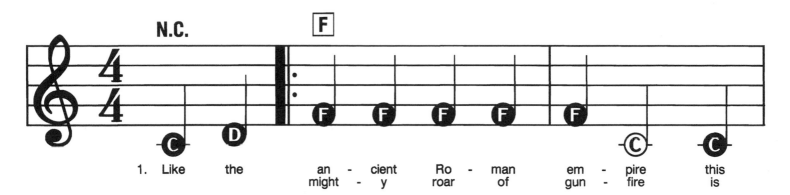

1. Like the an - cient Ro - man em - pire this
might - y roar of gun - fire is

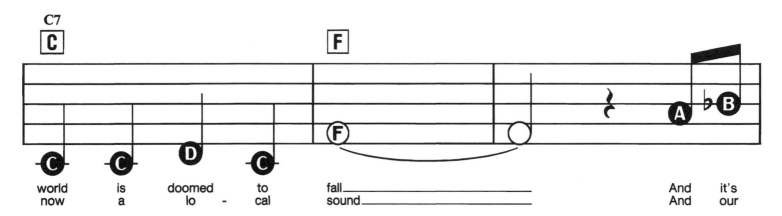

world is doomed to fall_____ And it's
now a lo - cal sound_____ And our

much too big a thing for mor - tal man._____
cit - y big streets are filled with an - gry men._____

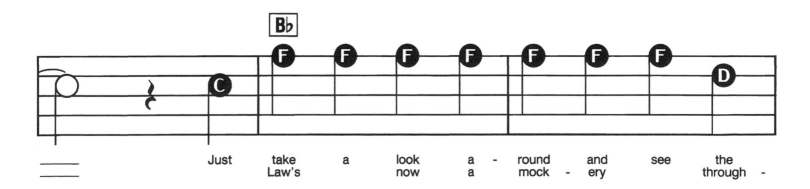

Just take a look a - round and see the
Law's now a mock - ery through -

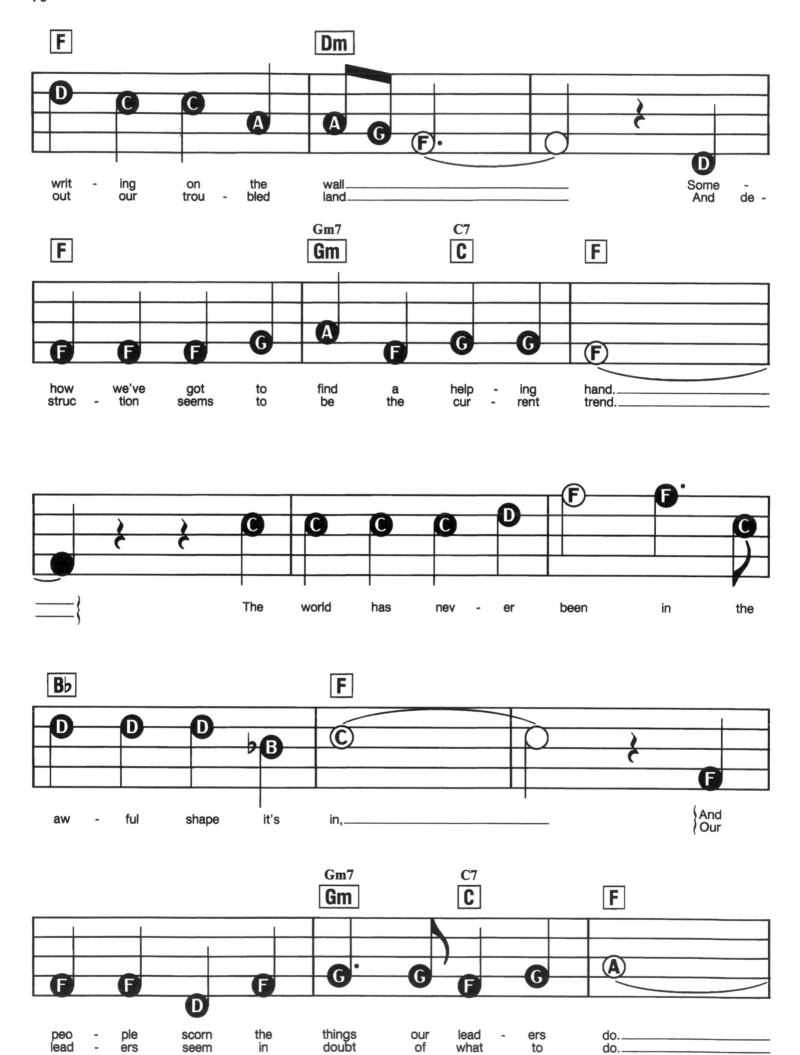

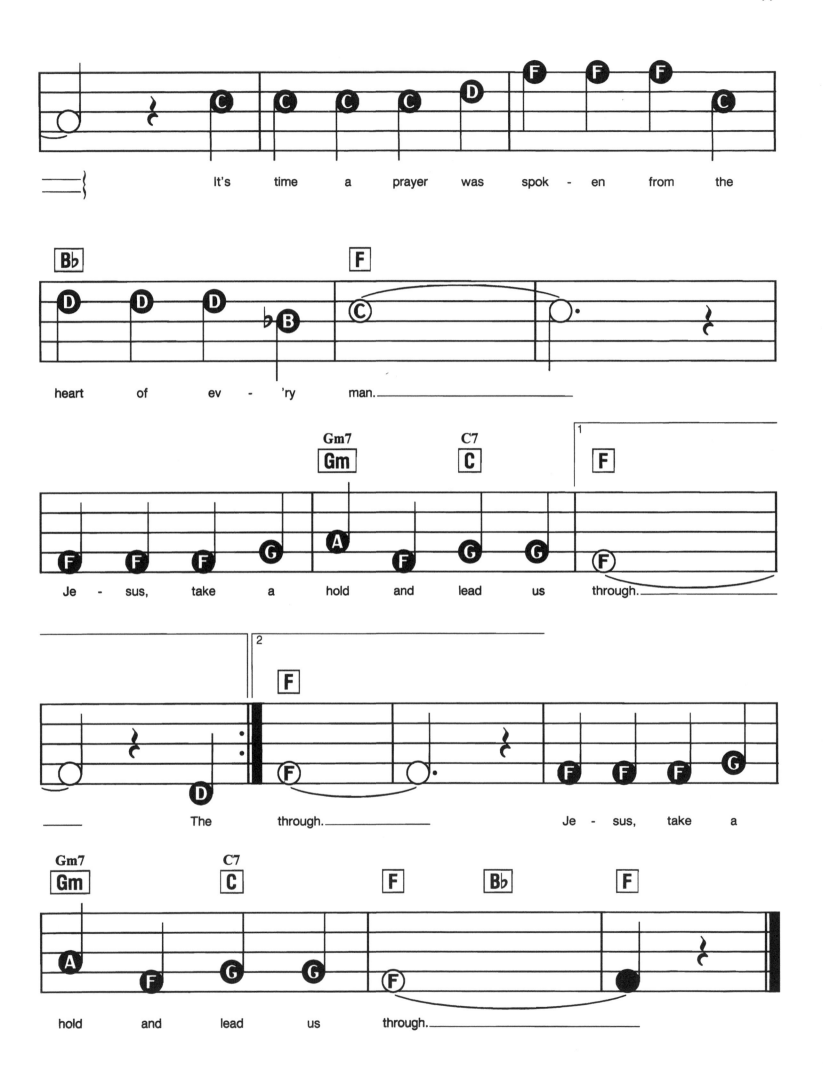

# The Legend of Bonnie and Clyde

Registration 9
Rhythm: Country or March

Words and Music by
Merle Haggard and Bonnie Owens

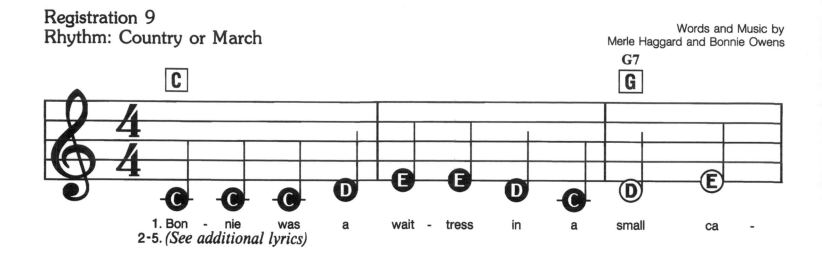

1. Bon - nie was a wait - tress in a small ca -
2-5. *(See additional lyrics)*

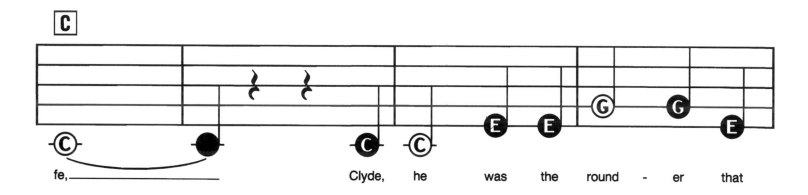

fe,_____ Clyde, he was the round - er that

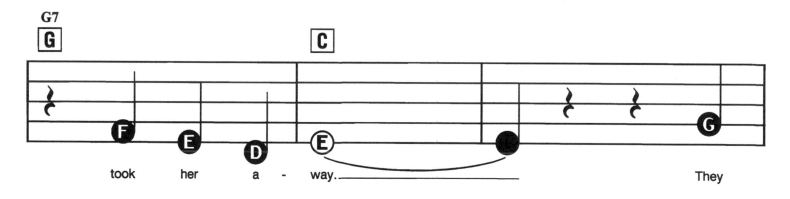

took her a - way._____ They

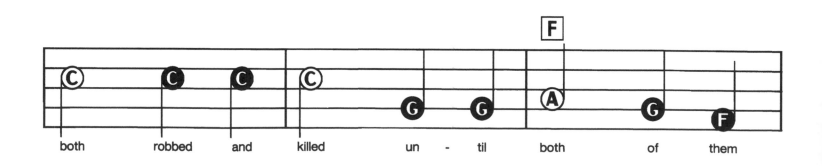

both robbed and killed un - til both of them

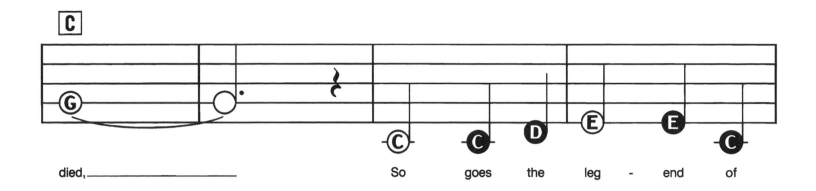

died,_____ So goes the leg - end of

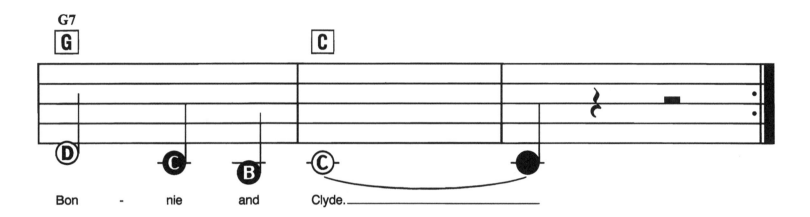

Bon - nie and Clyde._____

## Additional Lyrics

2. The poem that she wrote of the life that they led
Told of the lawmen left dying or dead,
Some say that Clyde made her life a shame,
But the legend made Bonnie the head of the game.

3. The rampage grew wilder with each passing day,
The odds growing smaller with each get-away
With the end growing closer, the harder they fought,
With blood on their hands they were bound to get caught.

4. They drove back from town on one bright summer day,
When a man they befriended stepped out in the way,
With no thought of dying they pulled to the side,
But death lay there waiting for Bonnie and Clyde.

5. Two years of running was ended that day,
For robbing and killing they both had to pay,
But we'll always remember how they lived and died,
So goes the legend of Bonnie and Clyde.

# Let's Chase Each Other Around The Room

**Registration 5**
**Rhythm: Shuffle or Swing**

Words and Music by Merle Haggard,
Freddy Powers and Sheril Rodgers

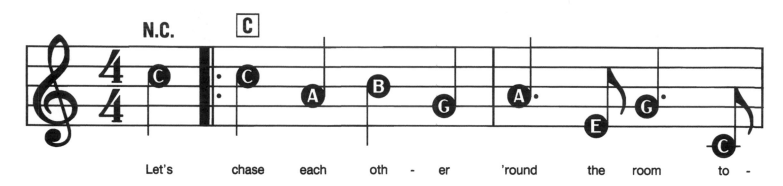

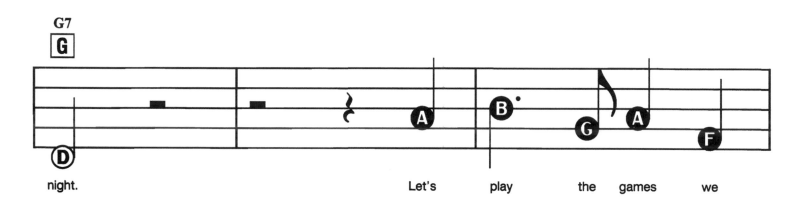

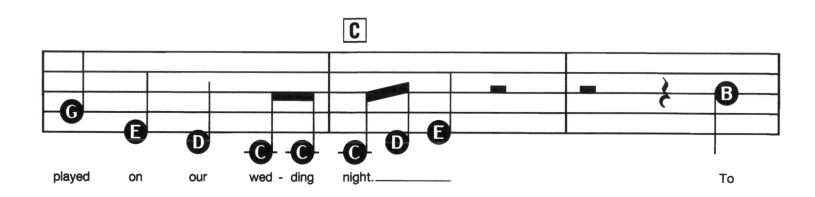

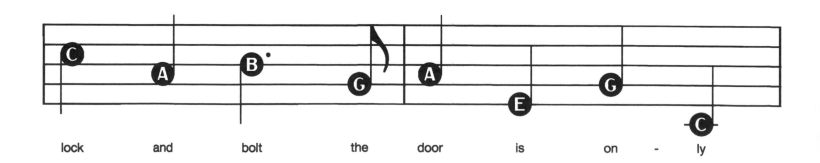

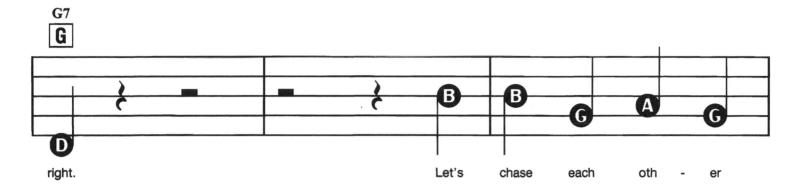

right.  Let's  chase  each  oth - er

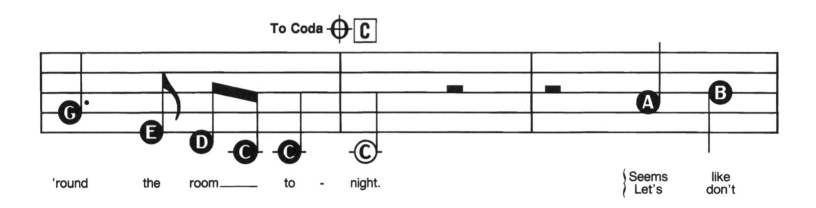

'round  the  room____  to - night.  { Seems  like  { Let's  don't

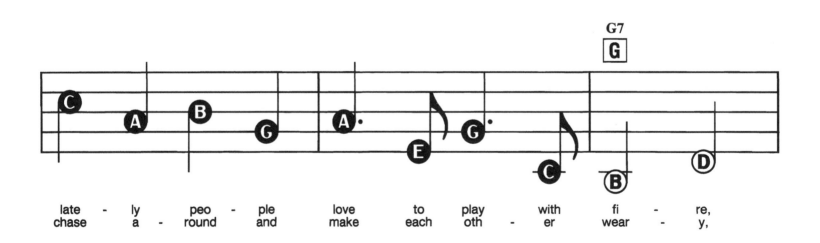

late - ly  peo - ple  love  to  play  with  fi - re,
chase  a - round  and  make  each  oth - er  wear - y,

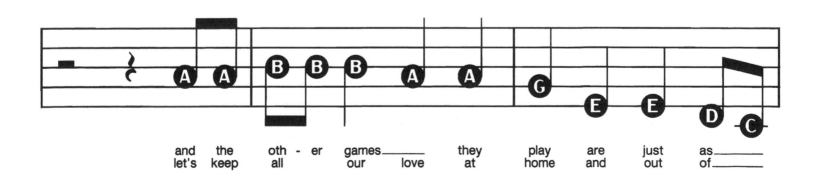

and  the  oth - er  games____  they  play  are  just  as____
let's  keep  all  our  love  at  home  and  out  of____

82

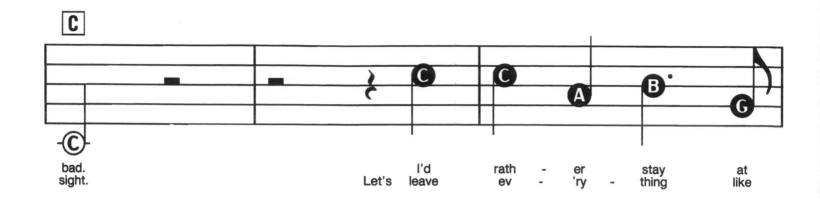

bad.
sight.  Let's I'd rath - er stay at
     leave ev - 'ry - thing like

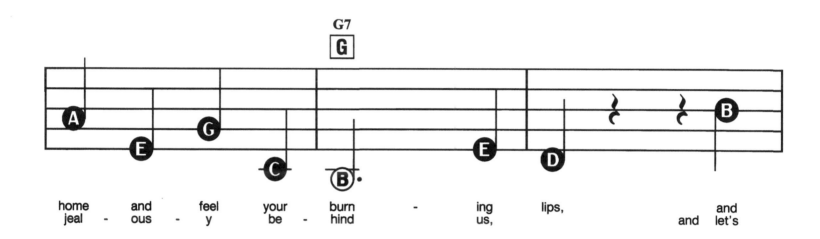

G7

home and feel your burn - ing lips,   and
jeal - ous - y be - hind us,   and let's

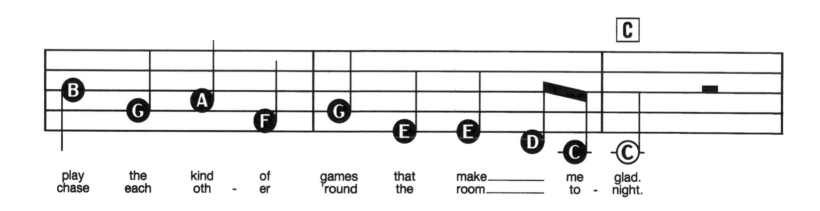

play the kind of games that make____ me glad.
chase each oth - er 'round the room____ to - night.

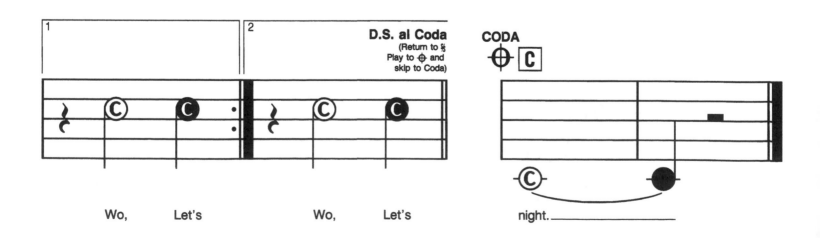

1

2    **D.S. al Coda**
    (Return to %
    Play to ⊕ and
    skip to Coda)

**CODA**

Wo, Let's   Wo, Let's   night.____

# Me And Crippled Soldiers

Registration 4
Rhythm: Pops or Country

Words and Music by
Merle Haggard and Bonnie Owens

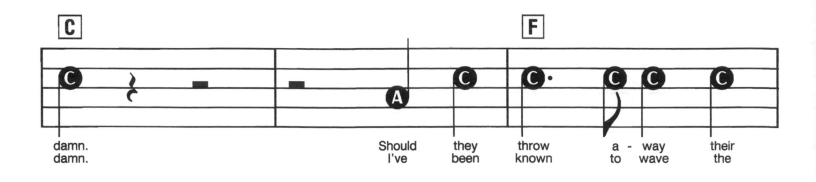
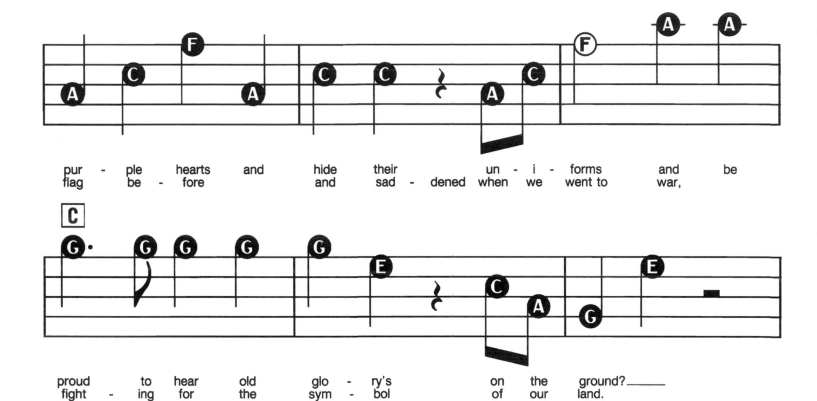
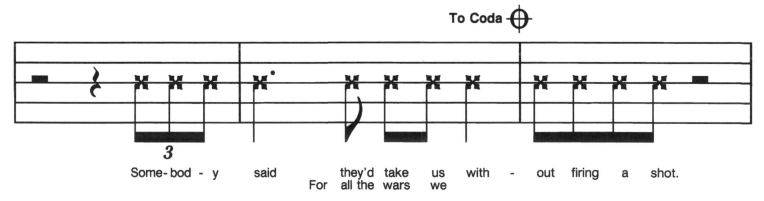
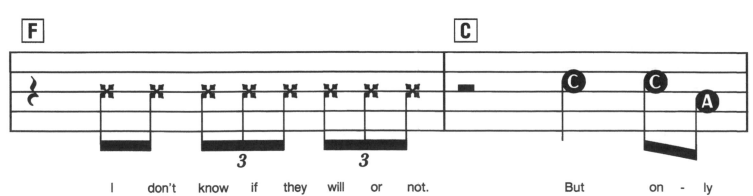

# Mama Tried

Registration 7
Rhythm: Rock or Country

Words and Music by
Merle Haggard

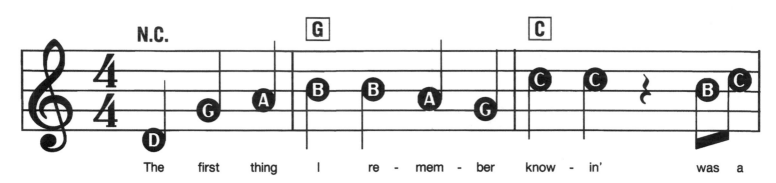

The first thing I re - mem - ber know - in' was a

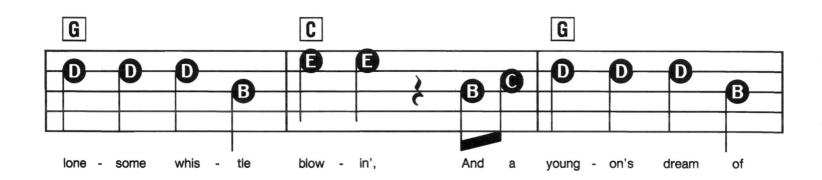

lone - some whis - tle blow - in', And a young - on's dream of

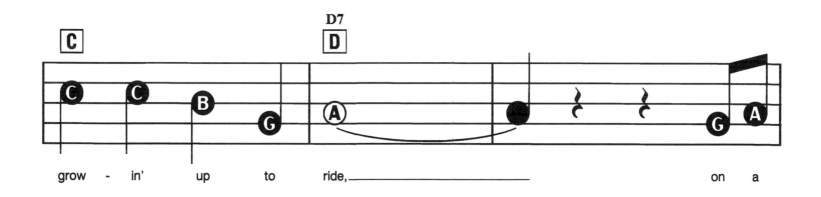

grow - in' up to ride,_____ on a

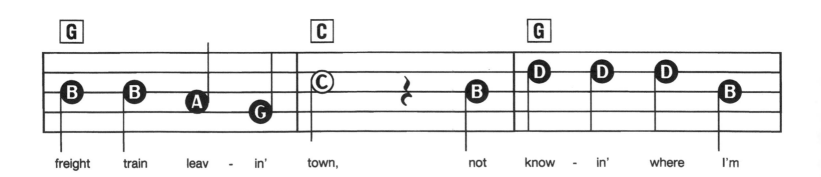

freight train leav - in' town, not know - in' where I'm

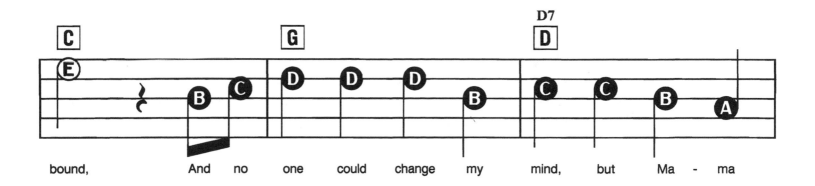

bound, And no one could change my mind, but Ma - ma

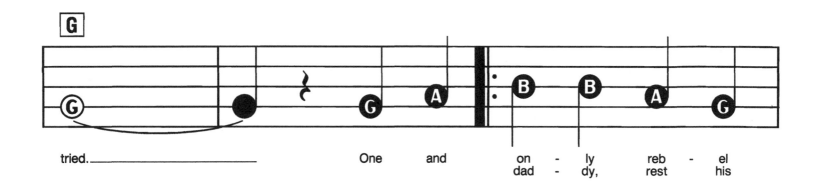

tried.____ One and on - ly reb - el
dad - dy, rest his

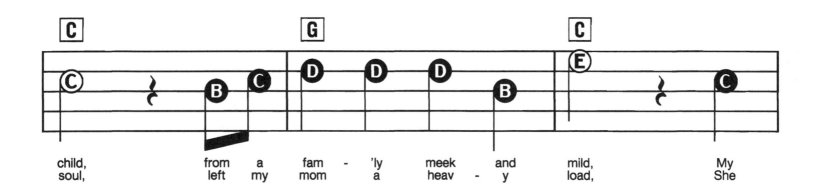

child, from a fam - 'ly meek and mild, My
soul, left my mom a heav - y load, She

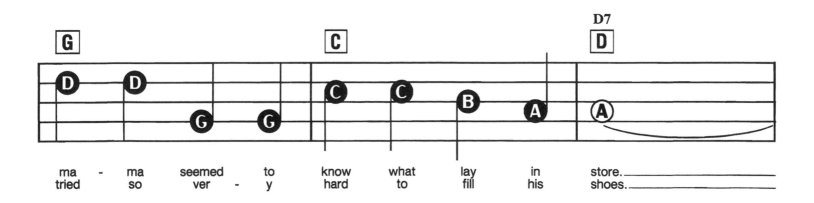

ma - ma seemed to know what lay in store.____
tried so ver - y hard to fill his shoes.____

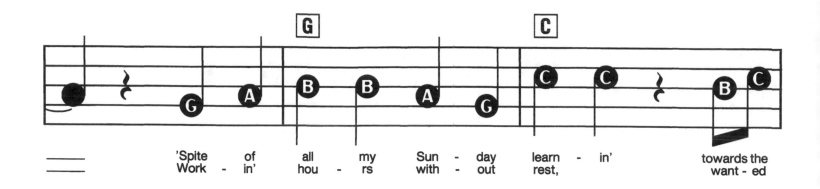

'Spite of all my Sun - day learn - in' towards the
Work - in' hou - rs with - out rest,          want - ed

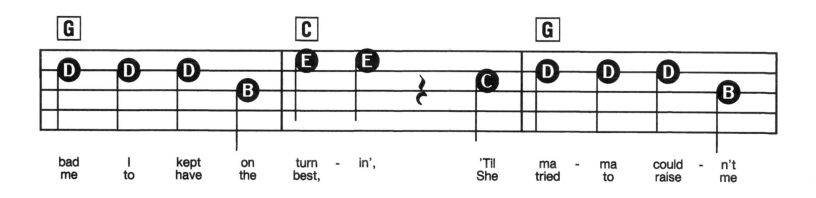

bad  I   kept  on   turn - in',   'Til ma - ma could - n't
me   to  have  the  best,        She tried to  raise   me

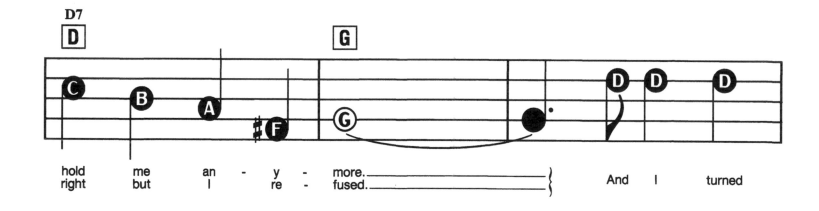

hold  me  an - y - more._____} And  I  turned
right me   I   re - fused._____}

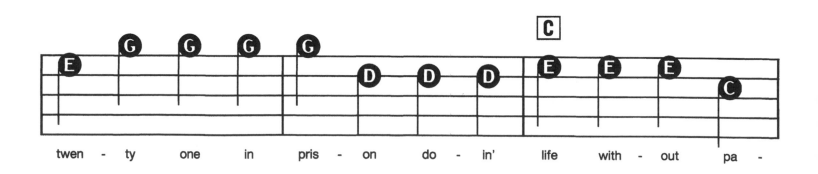

twen - ty one  in  pris - on do - in' life with - out pa -

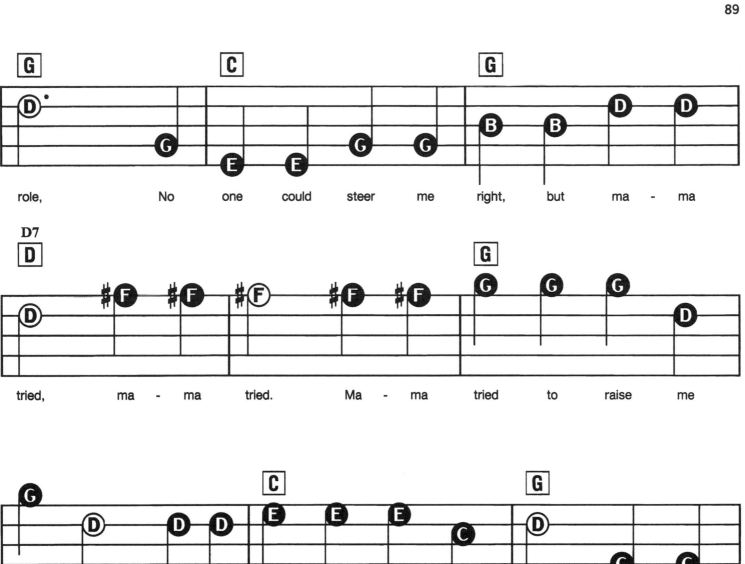

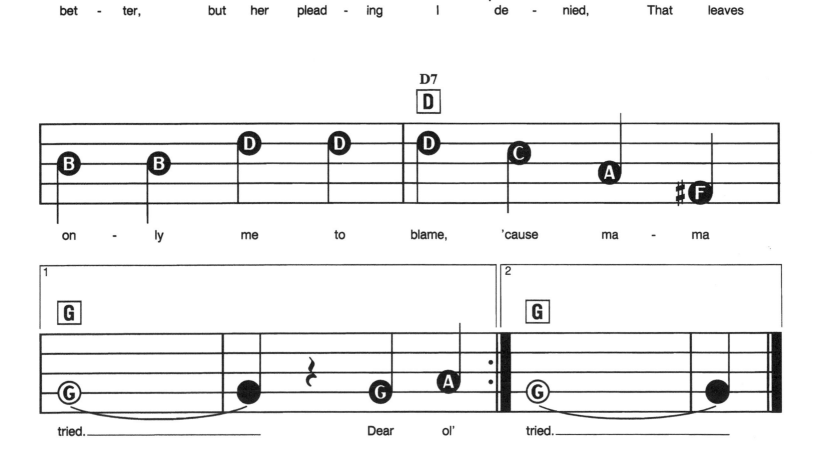

# Movin' On

Registration 9
Rhythm: Country or Shuffle

Words and Music by
Merle Haggard

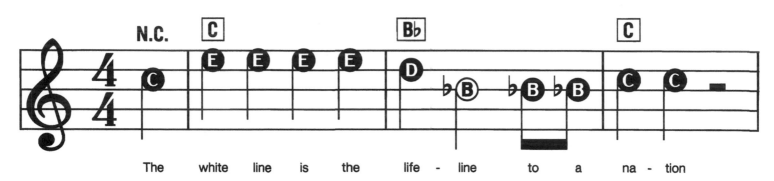

The white line is the life - line to a na - tion

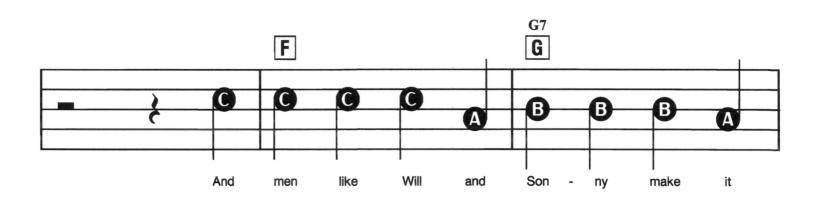

And men like Will and Son - ny make it

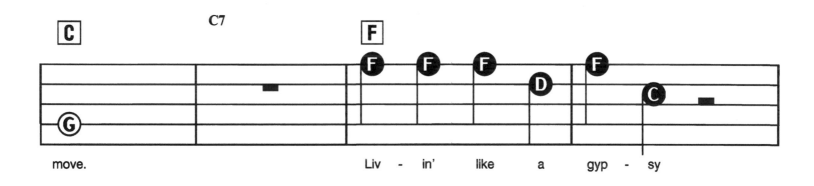

move. Liv - in' like a gyp - sy

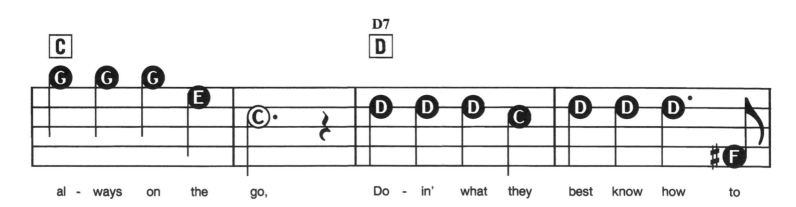

al - ways on the go, Do - in' what they best know how to

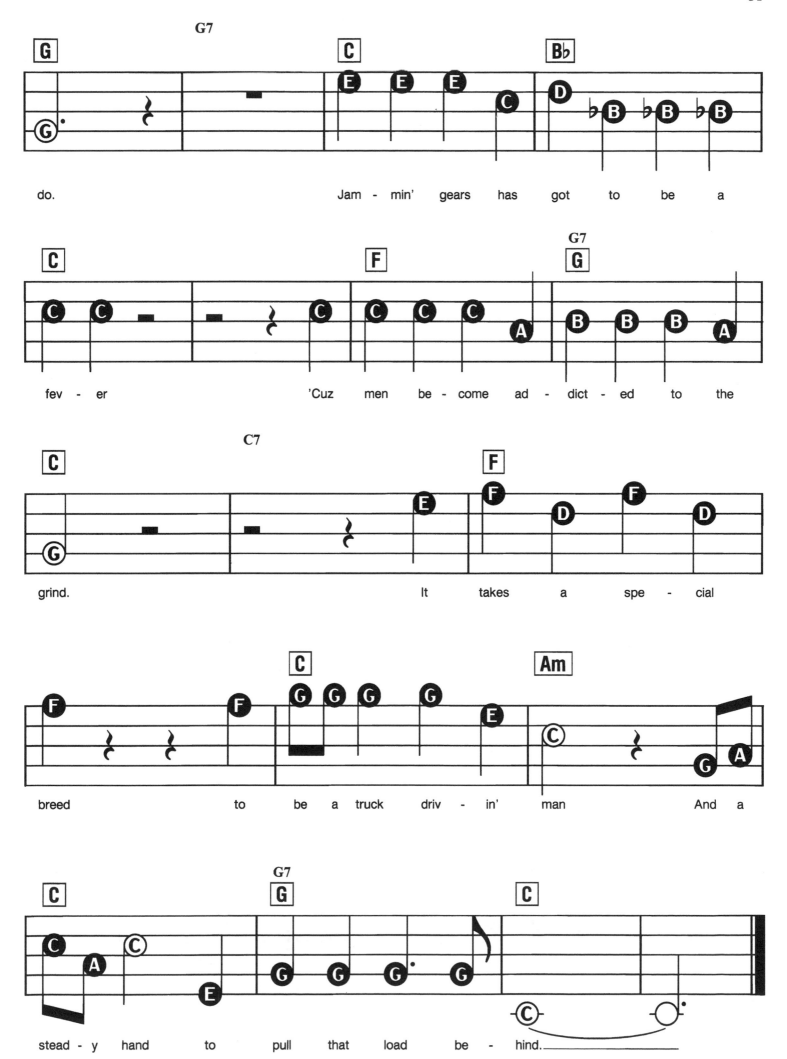

# My Favorite Memory

Registration 3
Rhythm: Waltz

Words and Music by
Merle Haggard

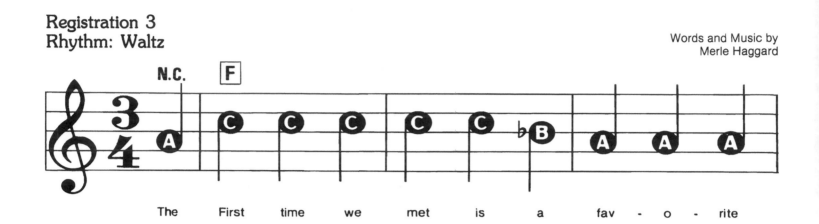

The First time we met is a fav - o - rite

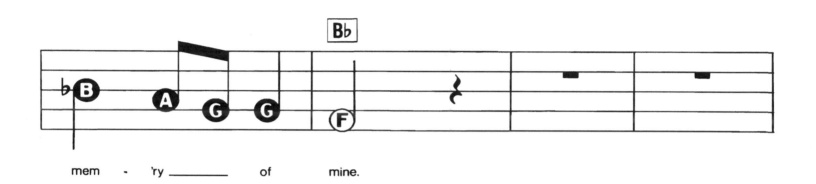

mem - 'ry _____ of mine.

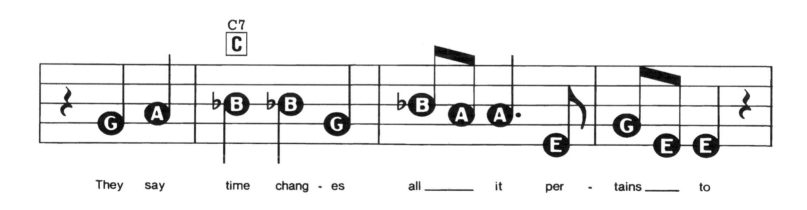

They say time chang - es all _____ it per - tains _____ to

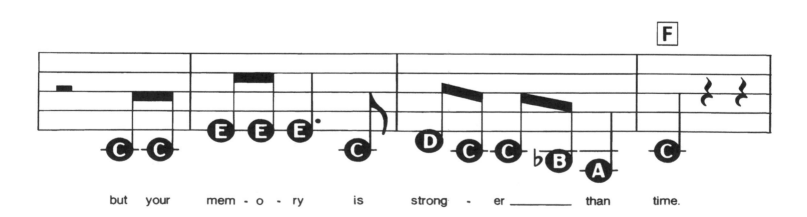

but your mem - o - ry is strong - er _____ than time.

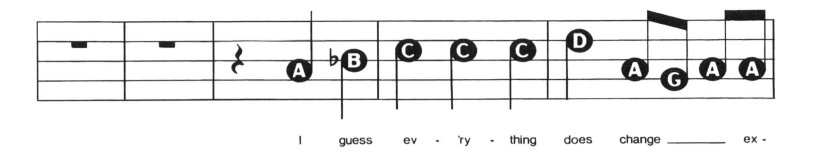

I guess ev - 'ry - thing does change _____ ex -

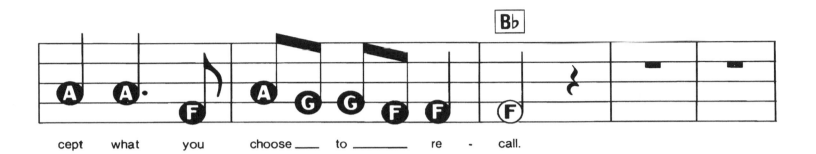

cept what you choose \_\_ to \_\_\_\_\_ re - call.

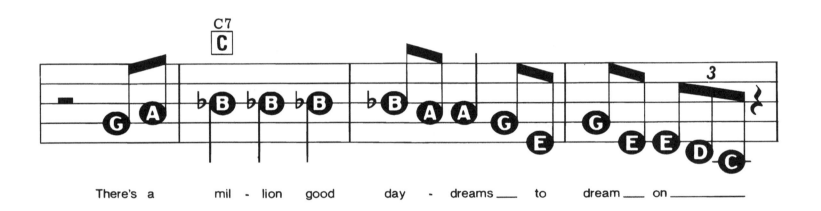

There's a mil - lion good day - dreams \_\_ to dream \_\_ on _____

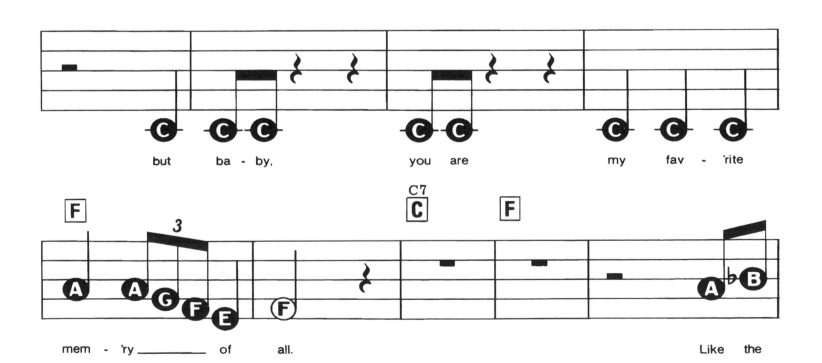

but ba - by, you are my fav - 'rite

mem - 'ry _____ of all.                          Like the

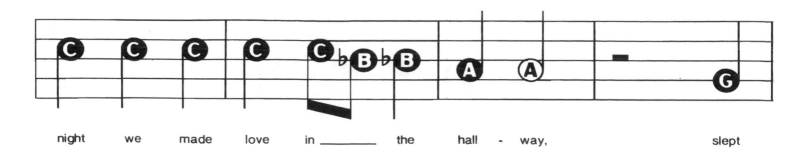

night   we   made   love   in _____ the   hall - way,        slept

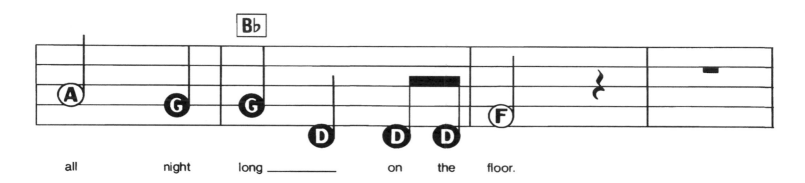

all      night    long _____    on    the    floor.

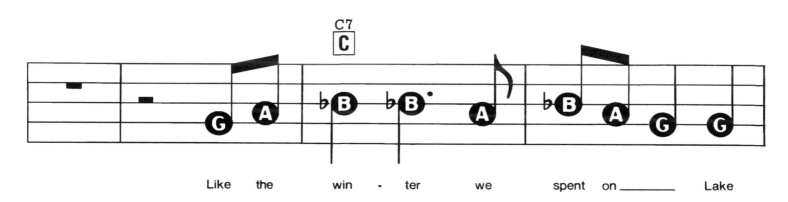

Like   the   win - ter   we   spent   on _____ Lake

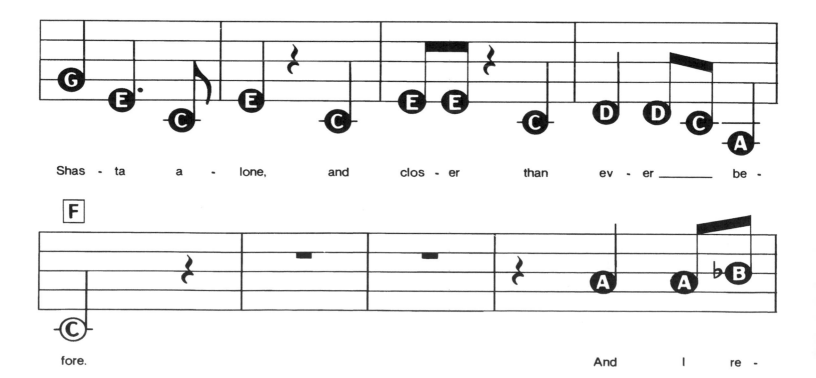

Shas - ta   a - lone,      and   clos - er   than   ev - er _____ be -

fore.                              And   I   re -

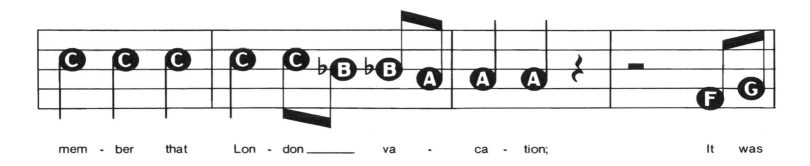

mem - ber that Lon - don _____ va - ca - tion; It was

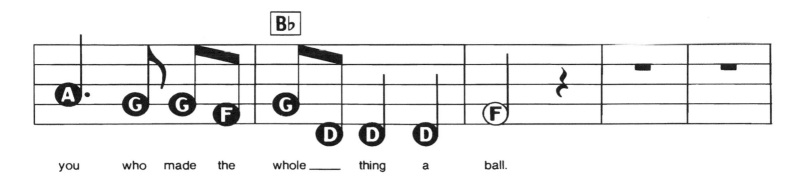

you who made the whole _____ thing a ball.

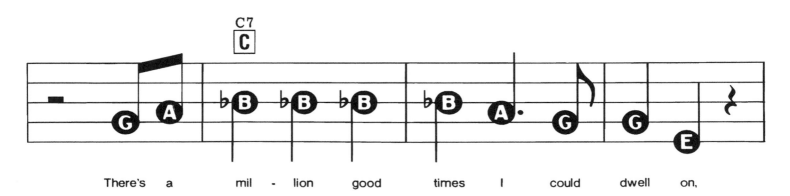

There's a mil - lion good times I could dwell on,

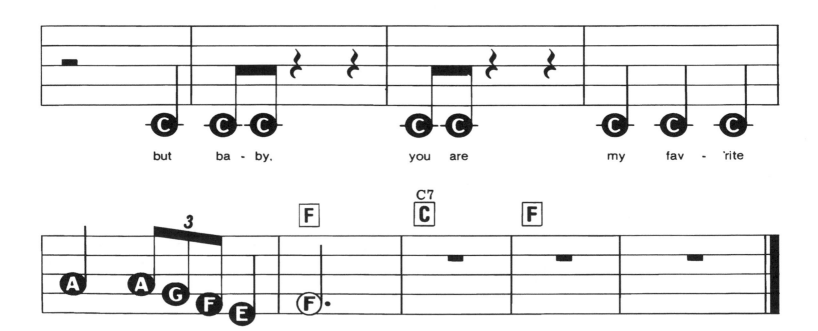

but ba - by, you are my fav - 'rite

mem - 'ry _____ of all.

# Natural High

Registration 7
Rhythm: Rock or Country

Words and Music by
Freddy Powers

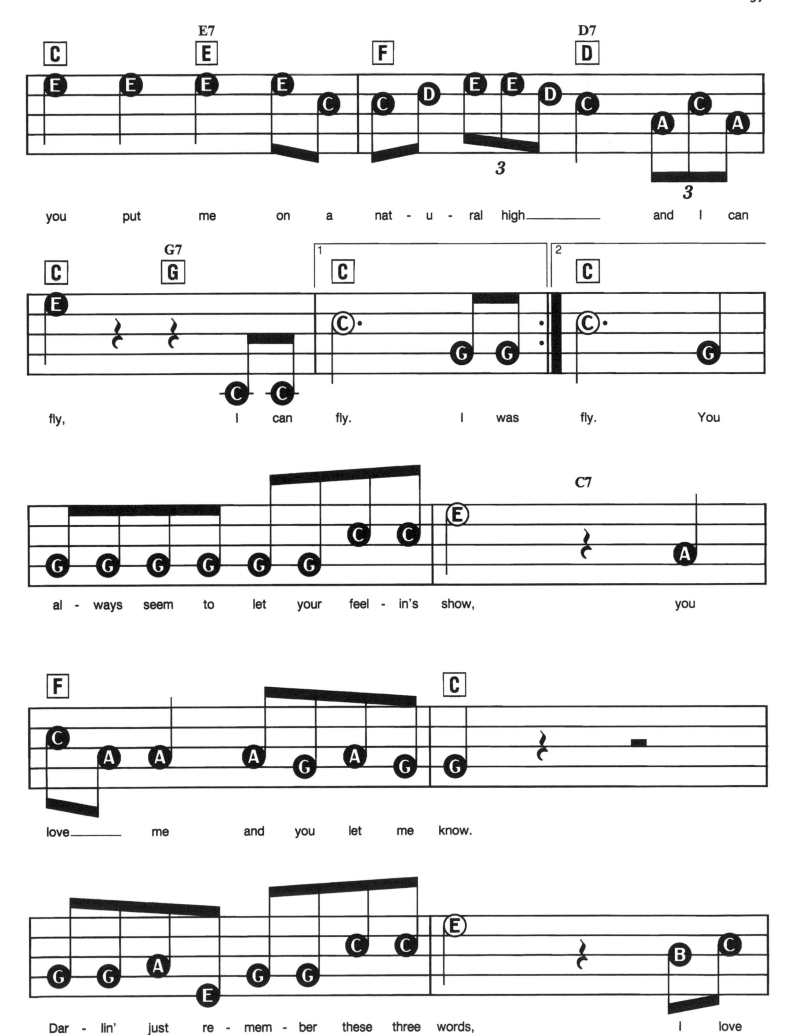

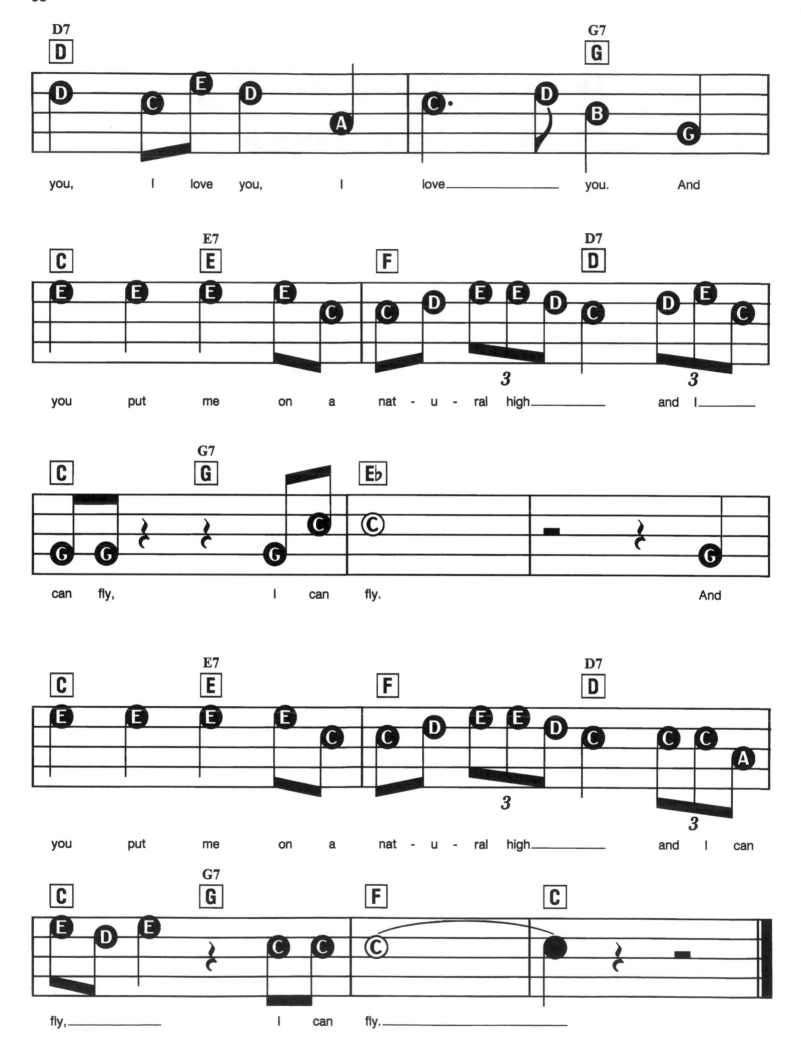

# Okie From Muskogee

Registration 4
Rhythm: Country or Shuffle

Words and Music by
Merle Haggard and Roy Edward Burris

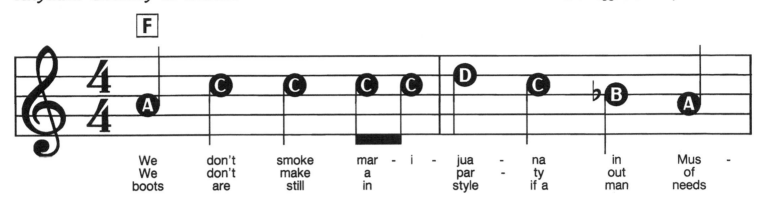

We don't smoke mar - i - jua - na in Mus -
We don't make a par - ty out of
boots are still in style if a man of

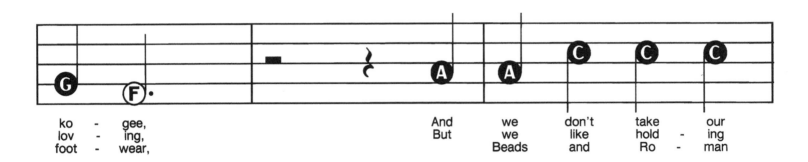

ko - gee, And we don't take our
lov - ing, But we don't like hold - ing
foot - wear, Beads and Ro - man

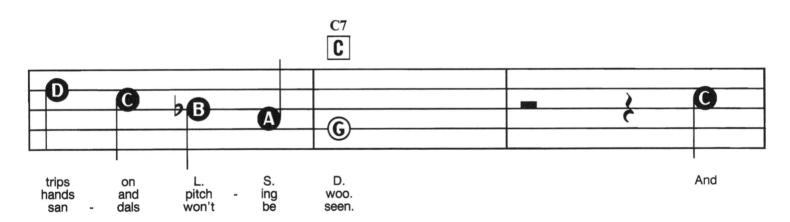

trips on L. S. D.
hands on and pitch - ing woo.
san - dals won't be seen. And

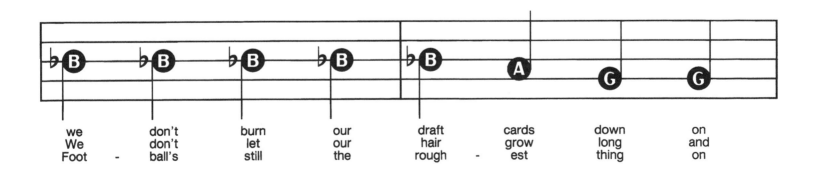

we don't burn our draft cards down on
We don't let our hair grow long and
Foot - ball's still the rough - est thing on

Main Street.
shag - gy
cam - pus,

But the we like liv - ing
Like the hip - pies out in
And the kids here still re -

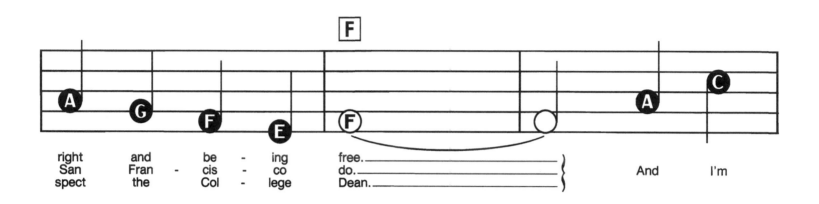

right and be - ing free.
San Fran - cis - co do.
spect the Col - lege Dean.

And I'm

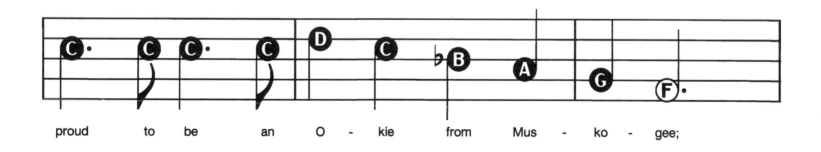

proud to be an O - kie from Mus - ko - gee;

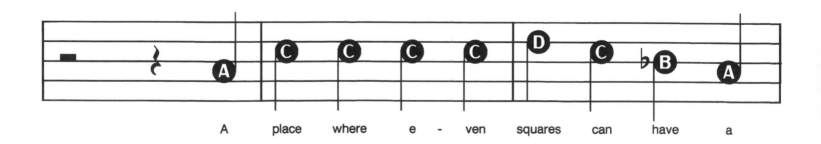

A place where e - ven squares can have a

101

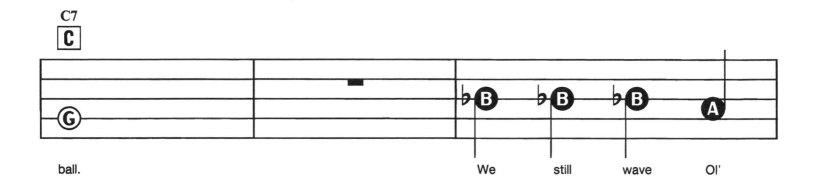

ball.             We   still   wave   Ol'

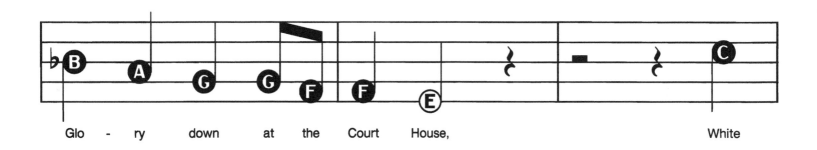

Glo - ry  down  at  the  Court  House,        White

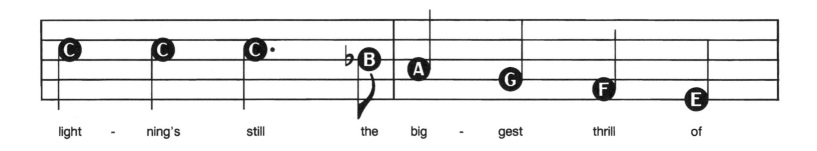

light - ning's  still   the  big - gest  thrill  of

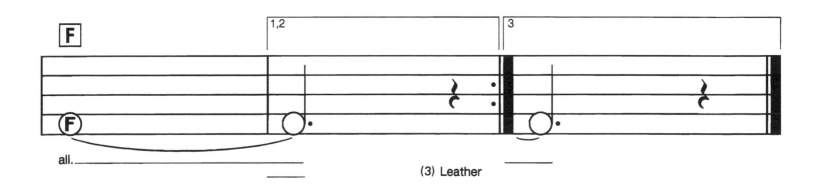

all.            (3) Leather

# Old Man From The Mountain

Registration 5
Rhythm: March or Country

Words and Music by
Merle Haggard

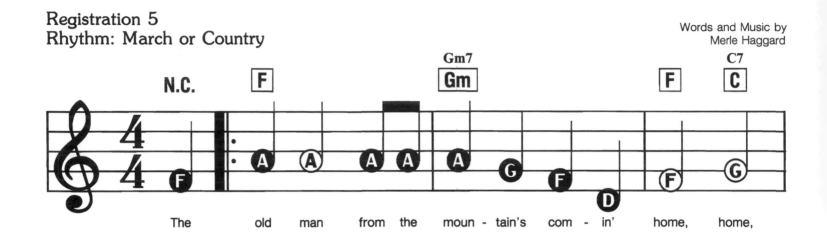

The old man from the moun - tain's com - in' home, home,

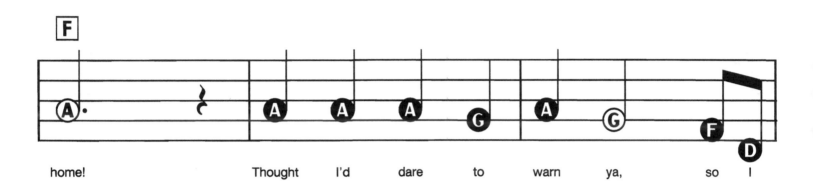

home! Thought I'd dare to warn ya, so I

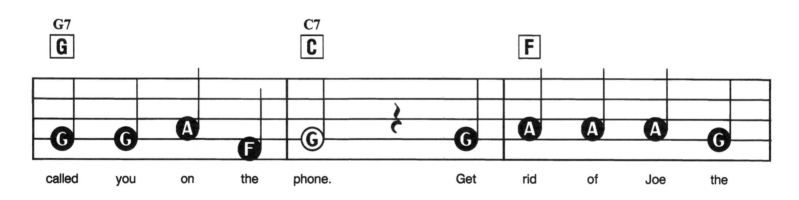

called you on the phone. Get rid of Joe the

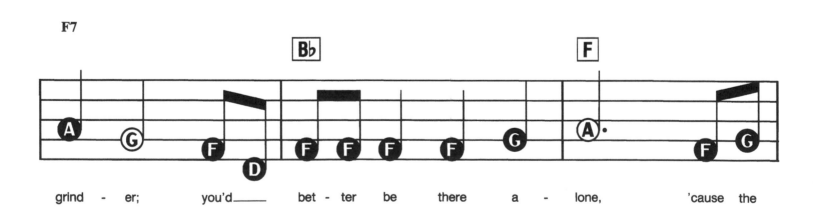

grind - er; you'd____ bet - ter be there a - lone, 'cause the

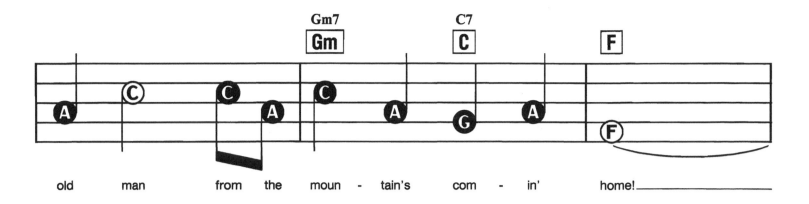

old man    from the    moun - tain's    com - in'    home!_____

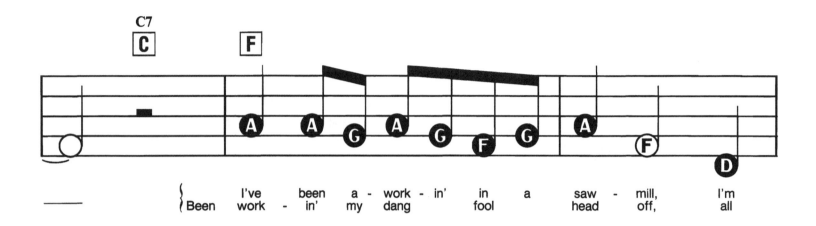

_____    {Been    I've    been    a - work - in'    in    a    saw - mill,    I'm
{Been    work - in'    my    dang    fool    head    off,    all

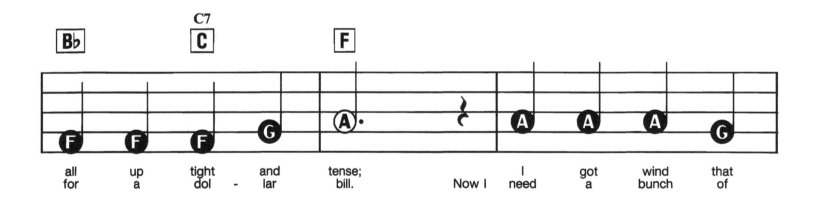

all    all    up    tight    and    tense;    Now I    I    got    wind    that
for    a    dol - lar    bill.    need    a    bunch    of

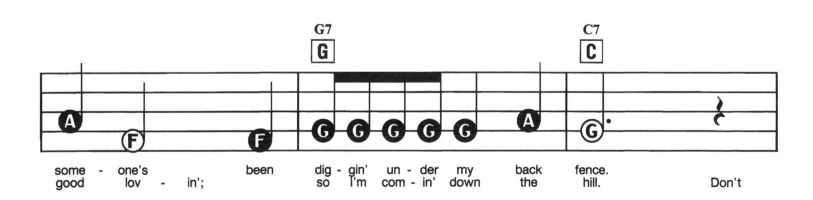

some - one's    been    dig - gin'    un - der    my    back    fence.    Don't
good    lov - in';    so I'm    com - in'    down    the    hill.

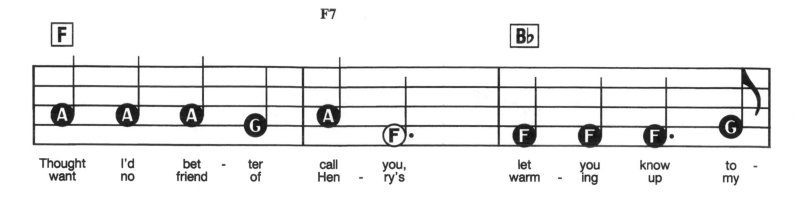

Thought I'd bet - ter call you, let you know to -
want no friend of Hen - ry's warm - ing up my

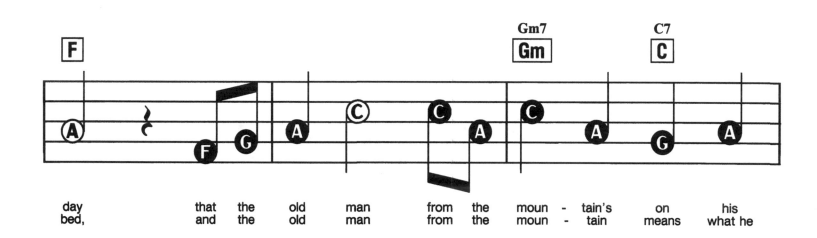

day that the old man from the moun - tain's on his
bed, and the old man from the moun - tain means what he

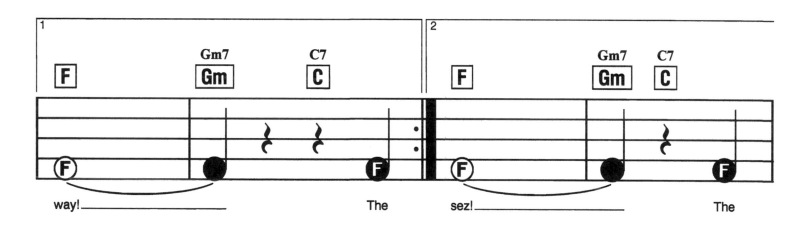

way!\_\_\_\_\_ The
sez!\_\_\_\_\_ The

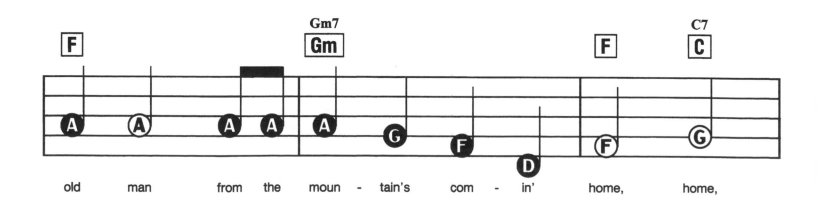

old man from the moun - tain's com - in' home, home,

105

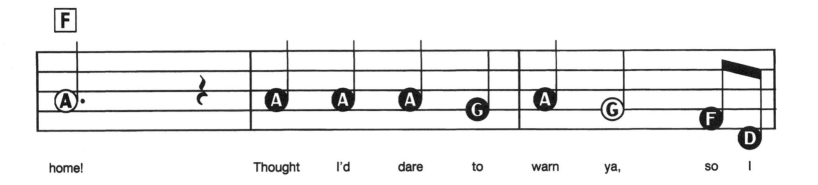

home! Thought I'd dare to warn ya, so I

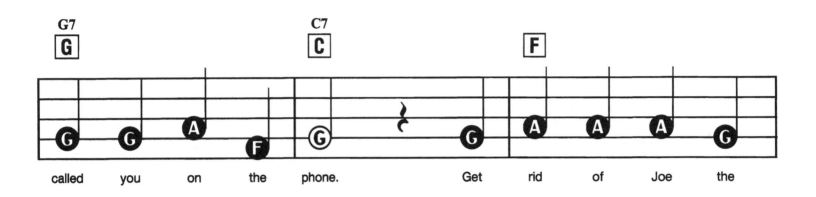

called you on the phone. Get rid of Joe the

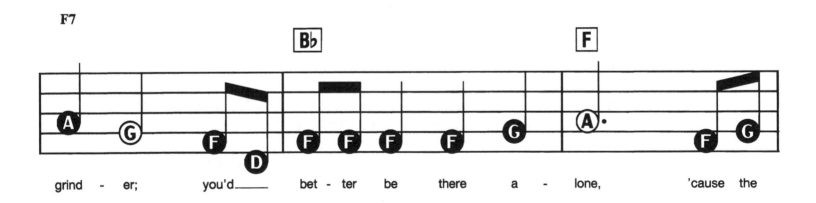

grind - er; you'd____ bet - ter be there a - lone, 'cause the

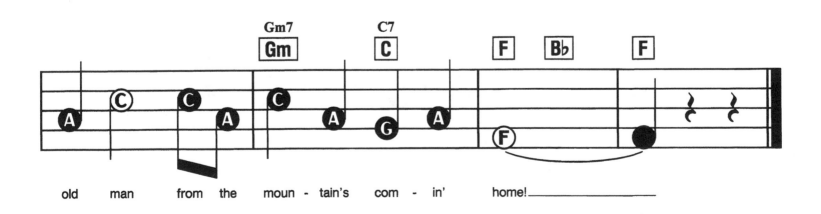

old man from the moun - tain's com - in' home!_____

# A Place To Fall Apart

Registration 7
Rhythm: Ballad or Country

Words and Music by Merle Haggard,
Willie Nelson and Freddy Powers

1. I'll prob - 'ly nev - er see you eye to eye
2. Write me back and tell me why it
3, 4. *(See additional lyrics)*

a - gain. This let - ter's meant to be my last fare -
end - ed, send a let - ter that I can last show my

well. But you need to un - der - stand I'm near - ly
heart. I'll be somewhere be - tween I love you and what you're

cra - zy, you need to know my life has gone to
feel - ing now, look - in' for a place to fall a -

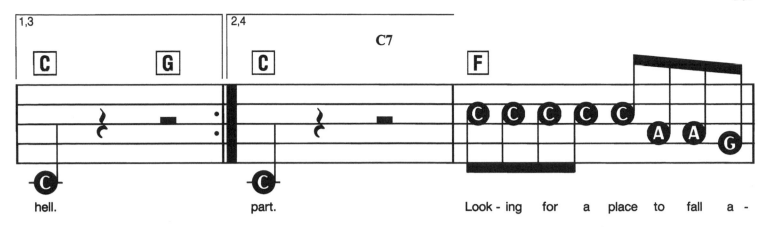

hell.　　　　　part.　　　　　Look - ing for a place to fall a -

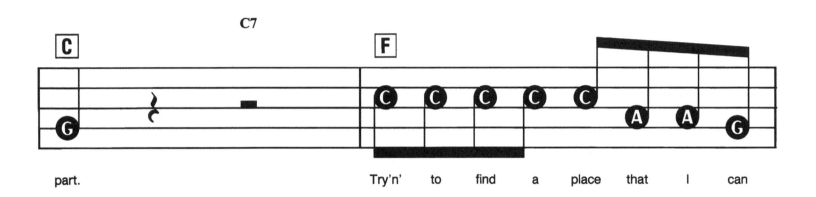

part.　　　　　Try'n' to find a place that I can

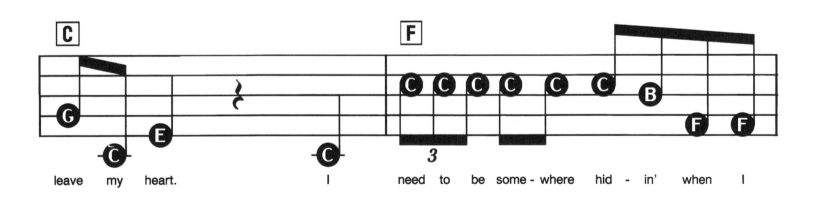

leave my heart.　　　　I　　need to be some - where hid - in' when I

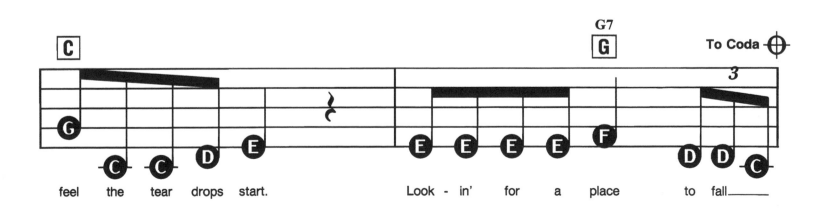

feel the tear drops start.　　　　Look - in' for a place to fall_____

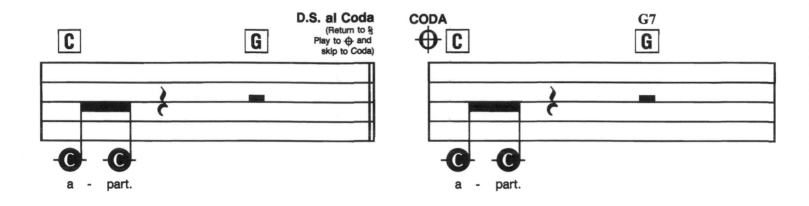

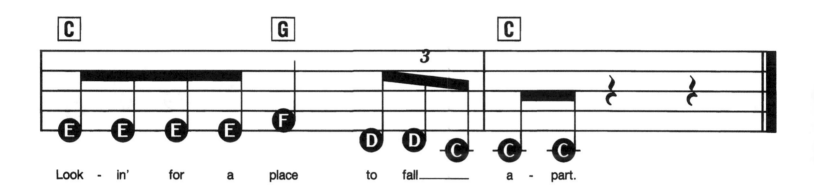

Additional Lyrics

3. I can't seem to justify your leavin' me,
I'm bewildered as to how it all came down.
I thought everything was fine until your phone call,
The call that turned my world upside down.

4. Send me word and tell me why it ended,
I need some final proof to show my heart.
I'll be somewhere between I love you and what you're feelin' now,
Lookin' for a place to fall apart.

# Rainbow Stew

Registration 4
Rhythm: Country or Shuffle

Words and Music by
Merle Haggard

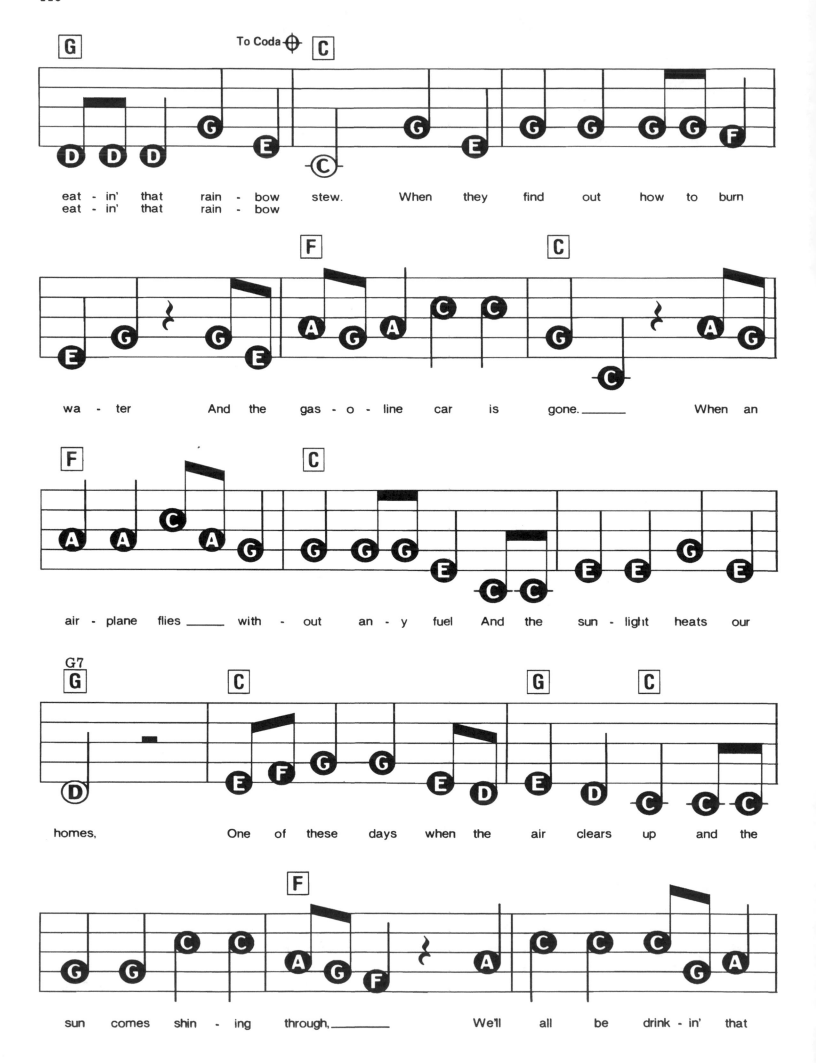

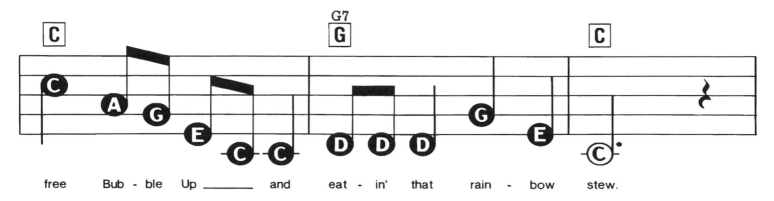

free  Bub - ble  Up _____ and  eat - in' that  rain - bow  stew.

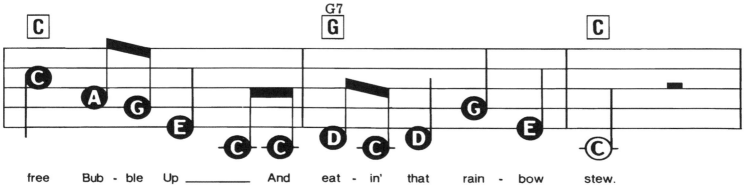

Eat - in'  rain - bow  stew  in  a  sil - ver  spoon ____ un - der -

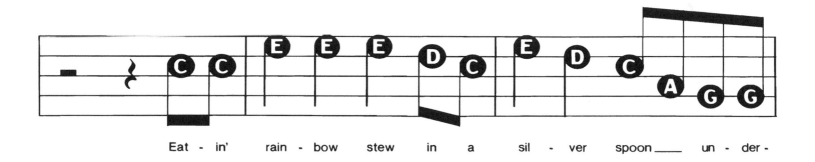

neath  those  skies  of  blue,  We'll  all  be  drink - in'  that

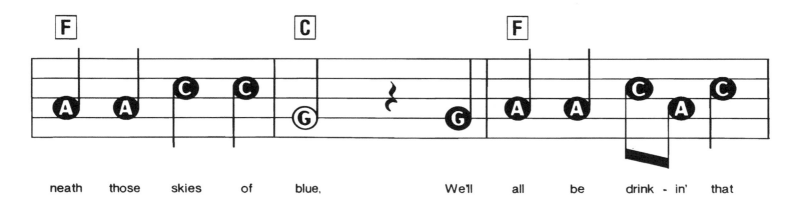

free  Bub - ble  Up _____ And  eat - in'  that  rain - bow  stew.

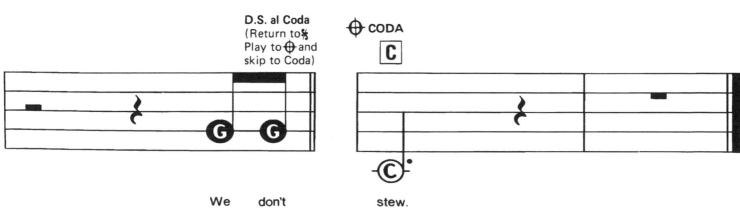

**D.S. al Coda**
(Return to %
Play to ⊕ and
skip to Coda)

⊕ CODA

We  don't                stew.

# Ramblin' Fever

Registration 4
Rhythm: Country or Shuffle

Words and Music by
Merle Haggard

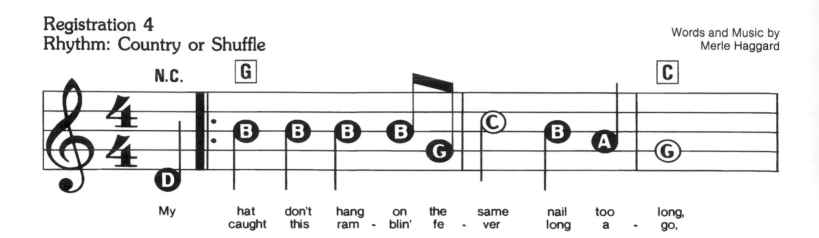

My     hat   don't  hang   on   the   same   nail   too   long,
caught this  ram -  blin'  fe - ver   long   a  -  go,

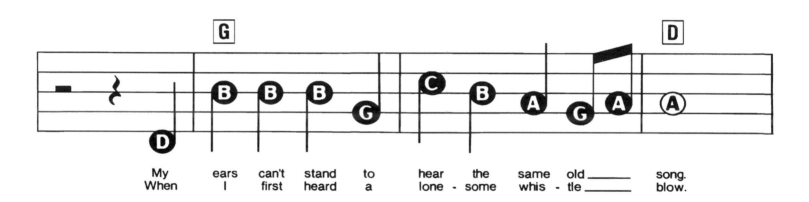

My     ears  can't  stand   to   hear   the   same  old _____ song.
When   I     first  heard   a    lone - some  whis - tle _____ blow.

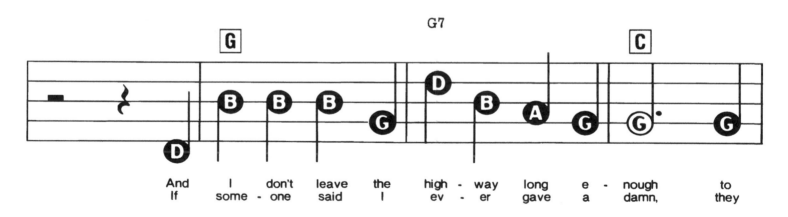

And    I     don't  leave   the   high - way  long   e - nough   to
If     some - one   said   I     ev  - er   gave   a   damn,   to   they

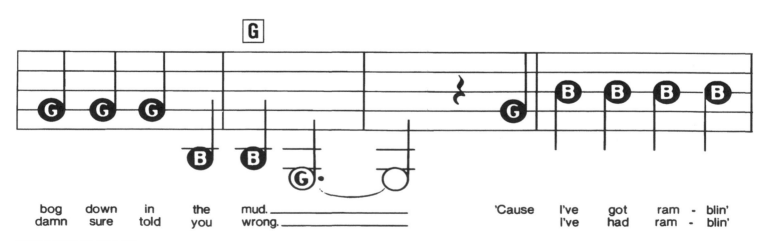

bog    down  in    the   mud. _____     'Cause  I've   got   ram - blin'
damn   sure  told  you   wrong. _____    I've   had   ram - blin'

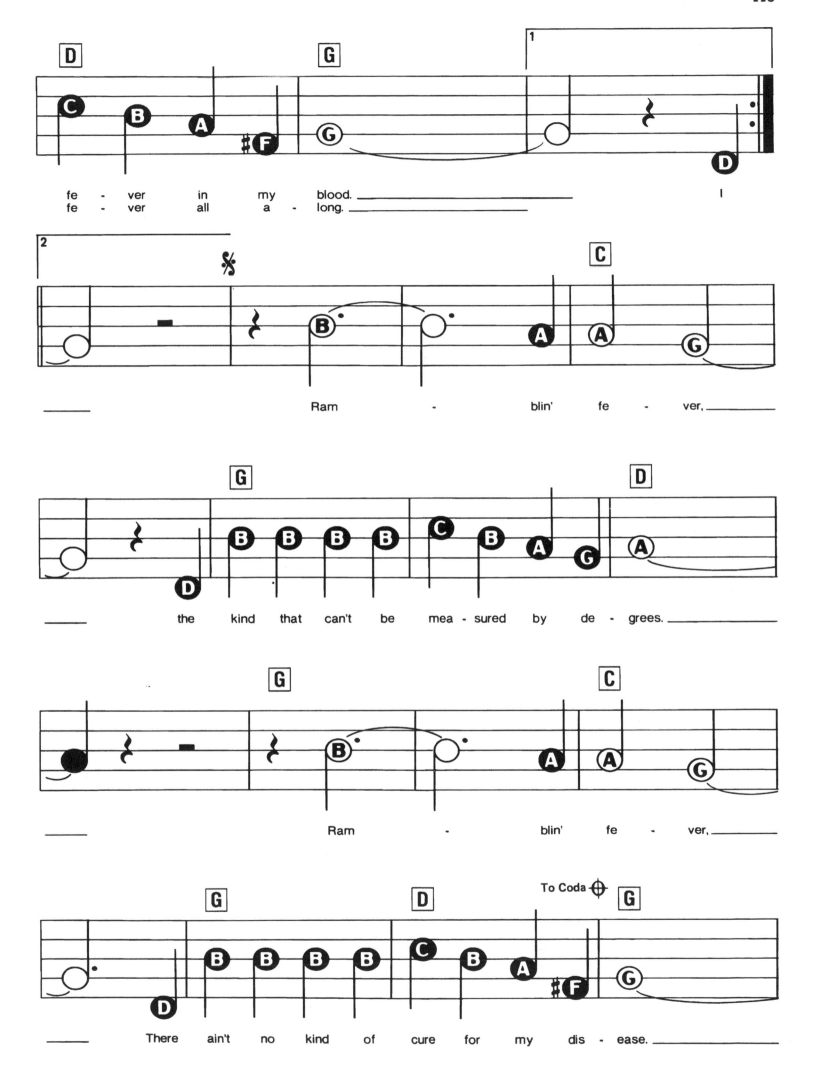

113

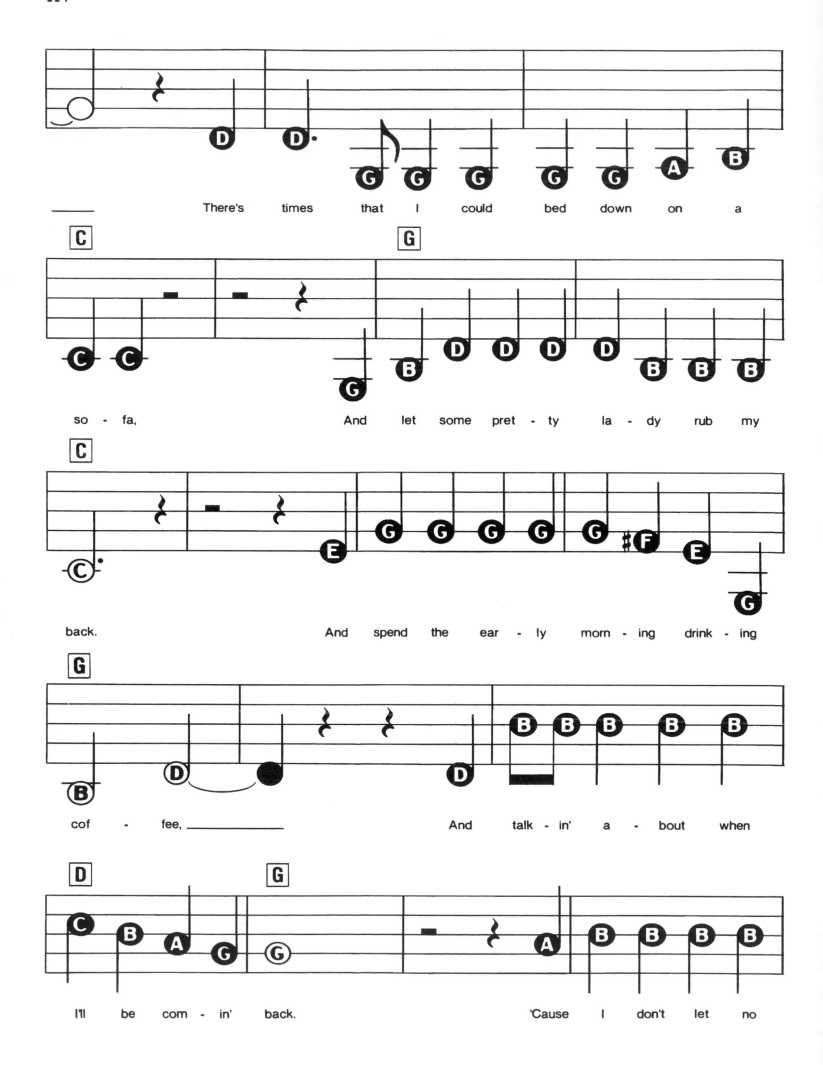

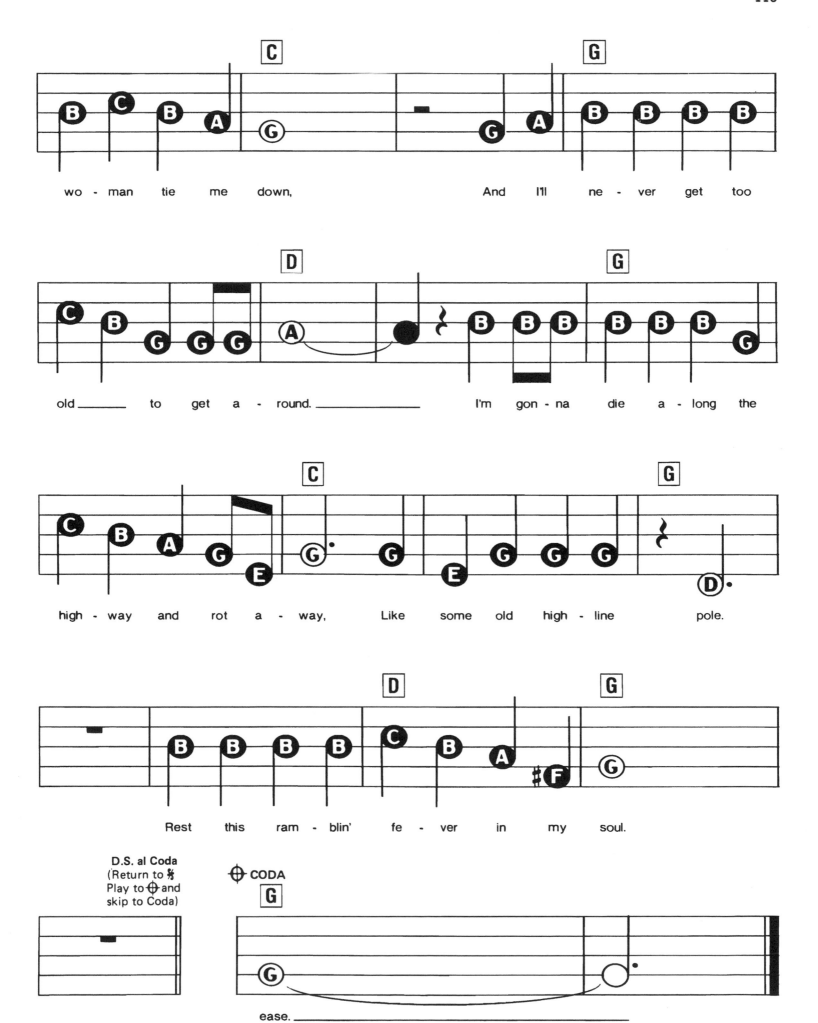

# Reasons To Quit

Registration 10
Rhythm: Country or Shuffle

Words and Music by
Merle Haggard

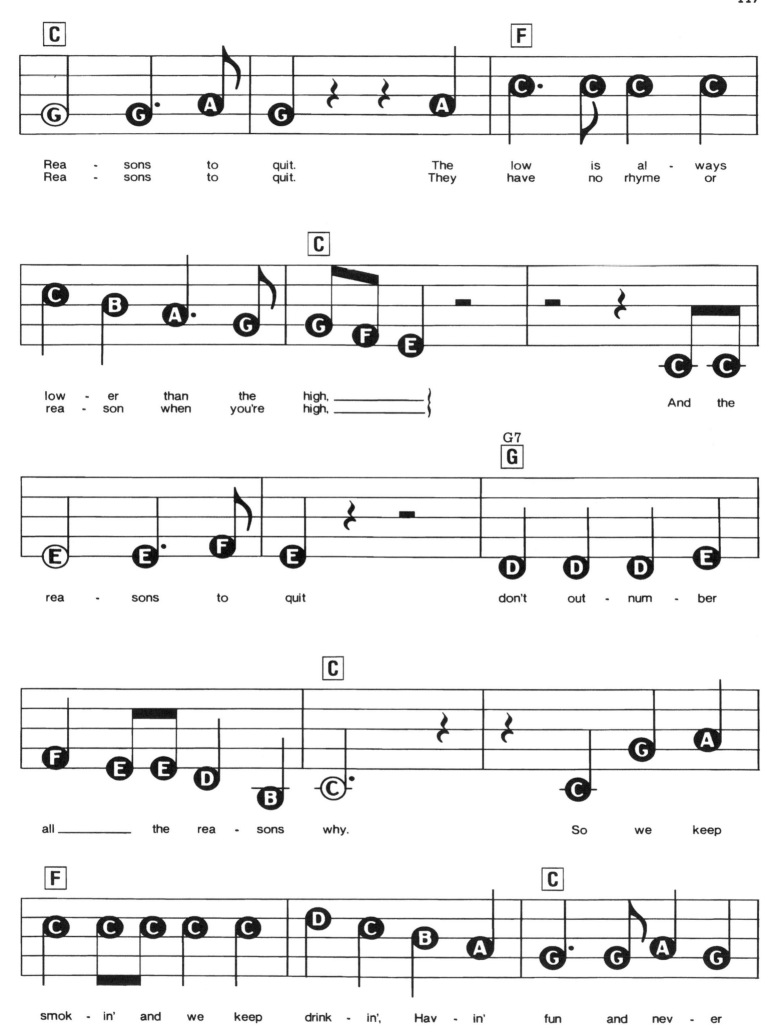

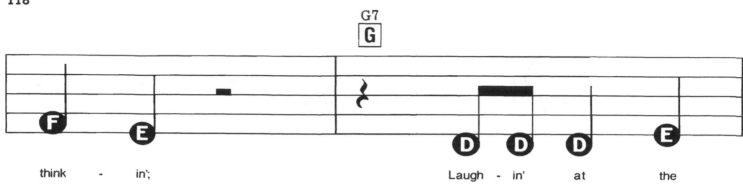

think - in';  Laugh - in' at the

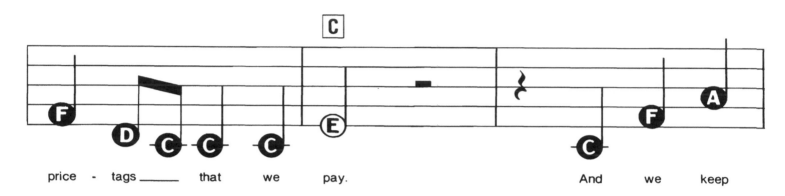

price - tags _____ that we pay.  And we keep

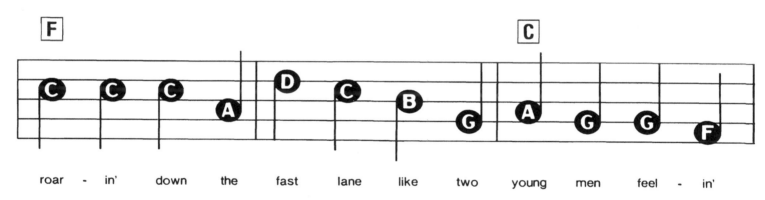

roar - in' down the fast lane like two young men feel - in'

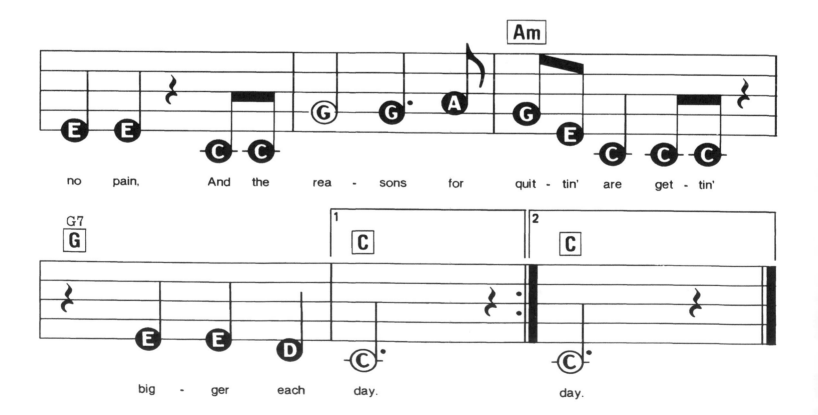

no pain,  And the rea - sons for quit - tin' are get - tin'

big - ger each day.  day.

# Red Bandana

Registration 5
Rhythm: Country or Shuffle

Words and Music by
Merle Haggard

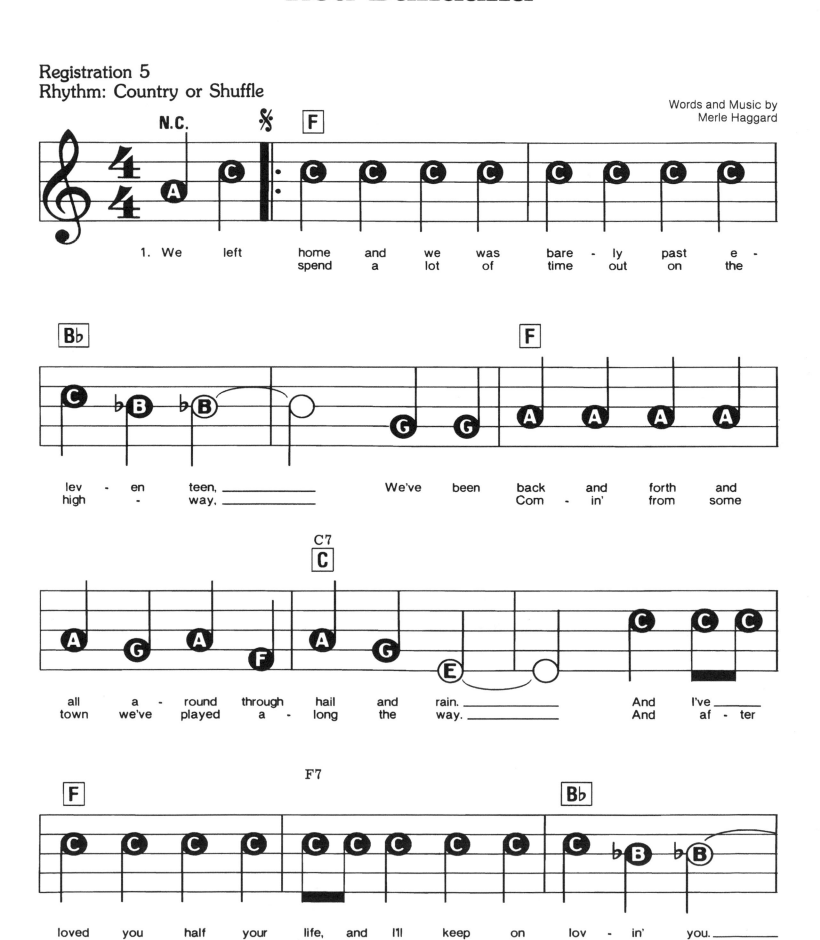

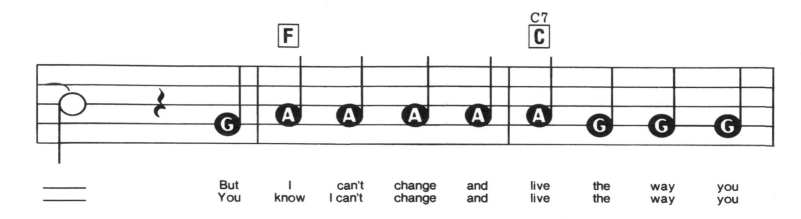

But    I    can't    change    and    live    the    way    you
You    know    I can't    change    and    live    the    way    you

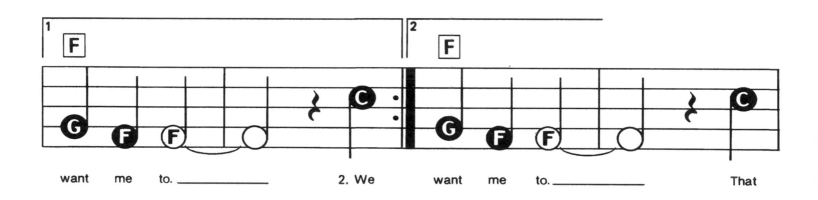

want    me    to. _____      2. We    want    me    to. _____      That

**Chorus**

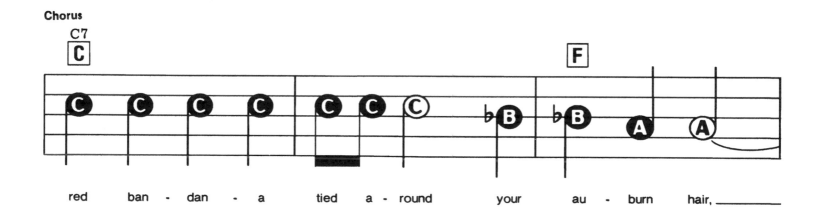

red    ban - dan - a    tied    a - round    your    au - burn    hair, _____

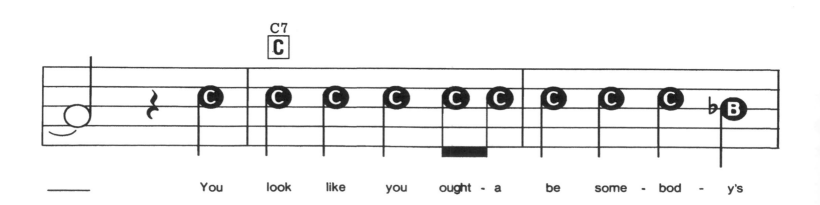

_____    You    look    like    you    ought - a    be    some - bod - y's

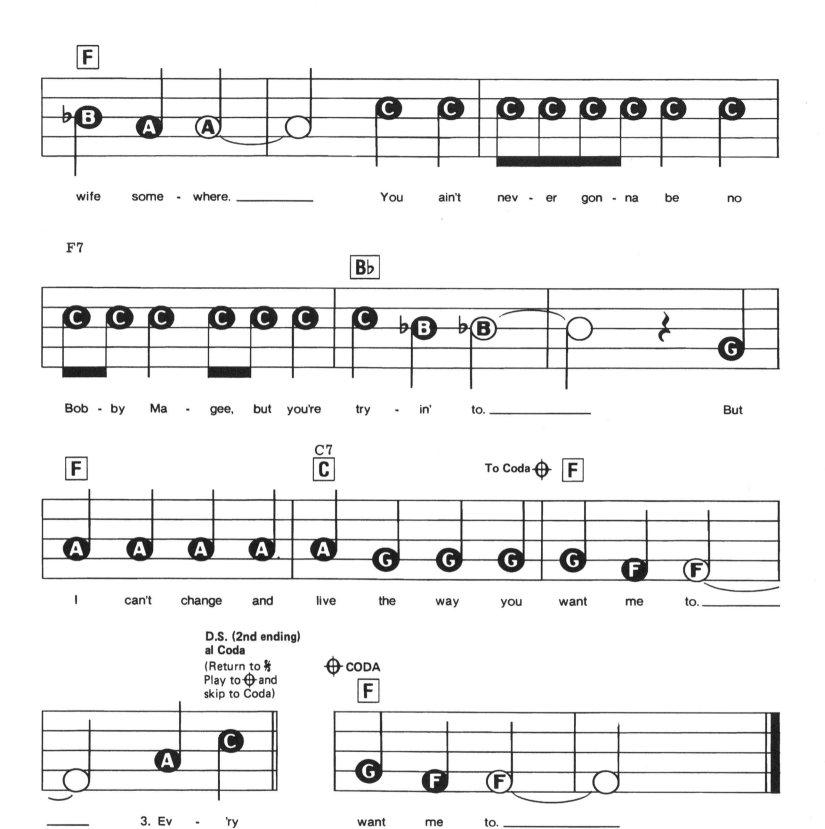

Verse 3. Ev'ry time you leave the stage I know you've had your fill,
And I wonder why you grew up and I never will.
Hey, I'm forty-one today, still goin' on twenty-two,
But I can't change and live the way you want me to.  That
(To Chorus)

# The Roots Of My Raising

Registration 8
Rhythm: Rock or 8 Beat

Words and Music by
Tommy Collins

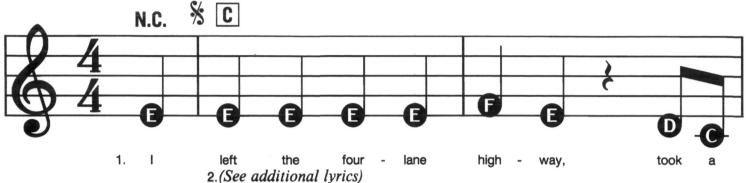

1. I left the four-lane high-way, took a
2. *(See additional lyrics)*

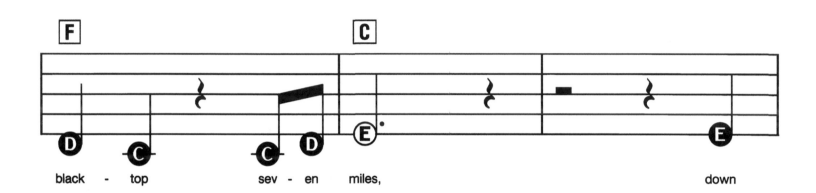

black-top sev-en miles, down

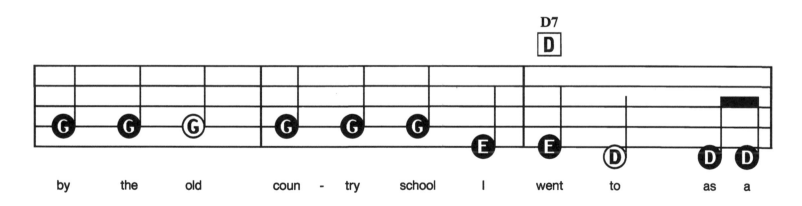

by the old coun-try school I went to as a

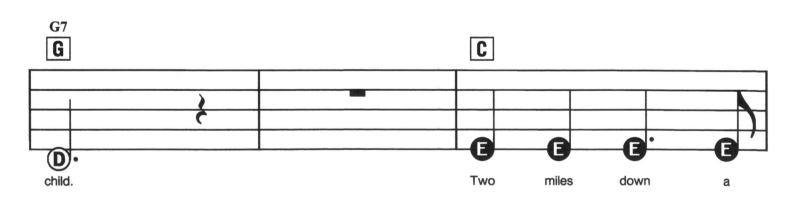

child. Two miles down a

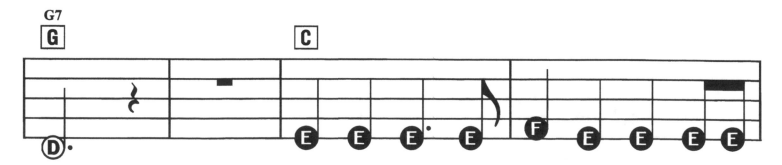

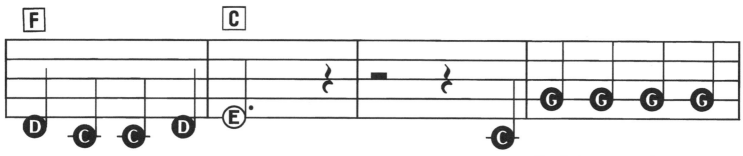

*I remembered how close they were.*      *So I just turned away.*

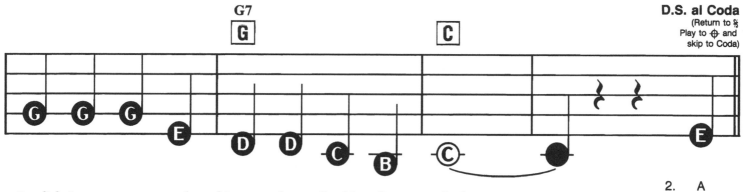

**D.S. al Coda**
(Return to ℅
Play to ⊕ and
skip to Coda)

*I didn't want to wake him and spoil his dream of her.*

2. A

**CODA**

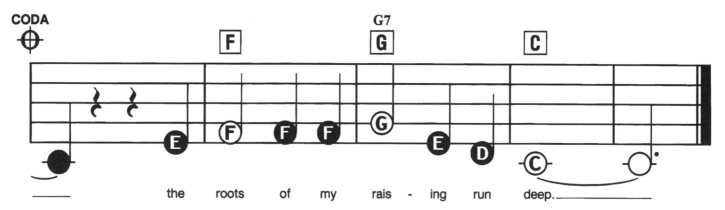

the roots of my rais - ing run deep.

Addtional Lyrics

2. A Christian mom who had the strength for life the way she did.
Then to pull that apron off and do the Charleston for us kids.
Dad, a quiet man who's gentle voice was seldom heard,
Could borrow money at the bank simply on his word.

(Repeat Chorus)

# Sing Me Back Home

Registration 3
Rhythm: Rock or 8 Beat

Words and Music by
Merle Haggard

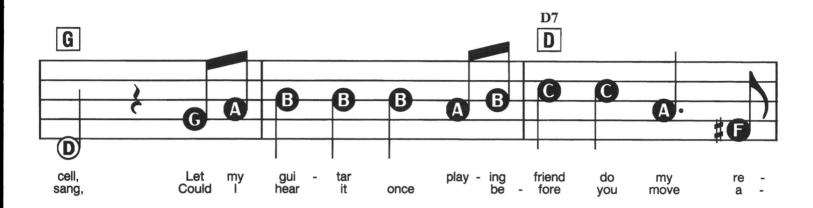

cell,      Let    my     gui - tar           play - ing    friend    do      my       re -
sang,     Could    I     hear      it     once         be - fore    you    move      a -

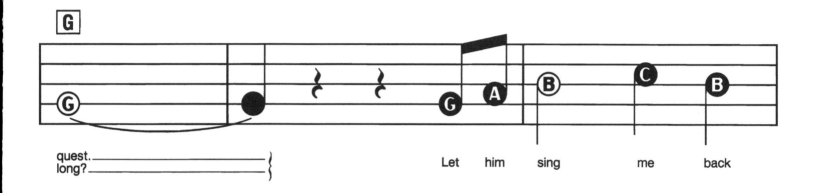

quest._____
long?_____                   Let    him    sing      me      back

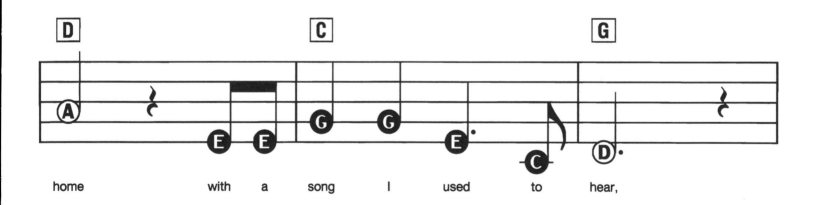

home        with     a     song     I     used      to     hear,

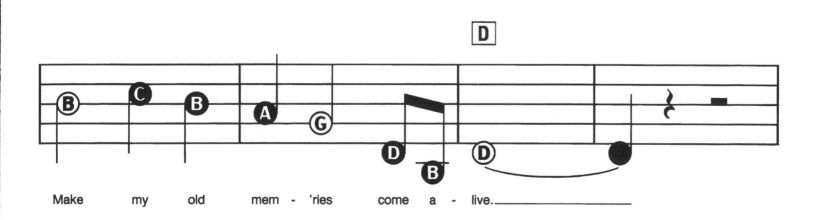

Make    my     old    mem - 'ries    come    a - live._____

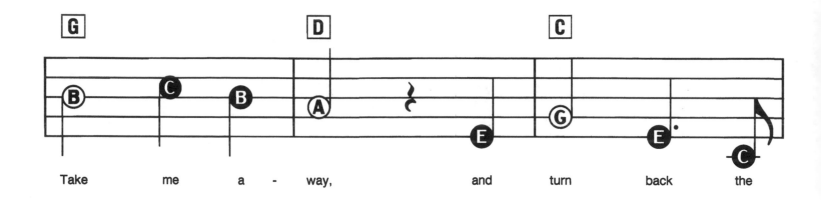

Take me a - way, and turn back the

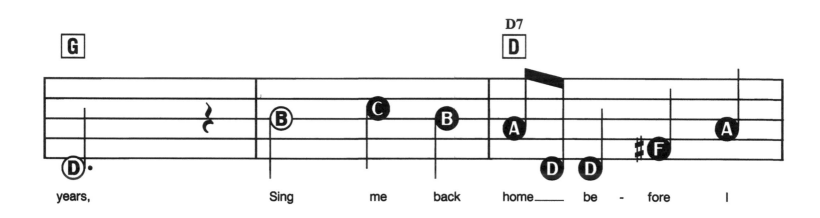

years, Sing me back home ____ be - fore I

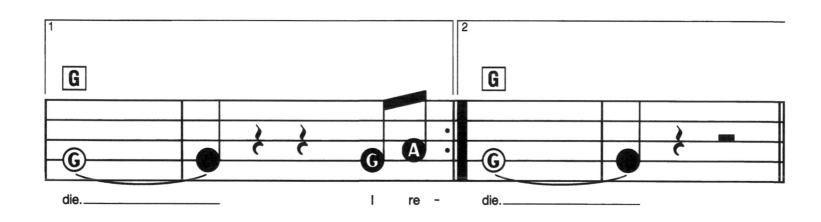

die. ____ I re - die. ____

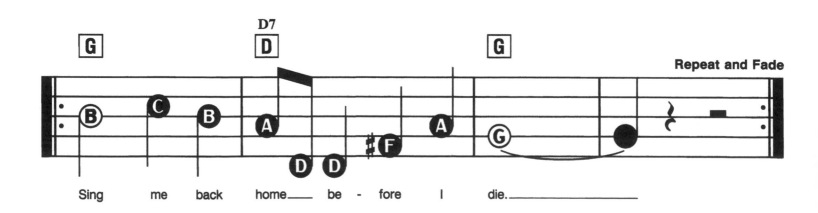

Sing me back home ____ be - fore I die. ____

# Swinging Doors

Registration 7
Rhythm: March or Country

Words and Music by
Merle Haggard

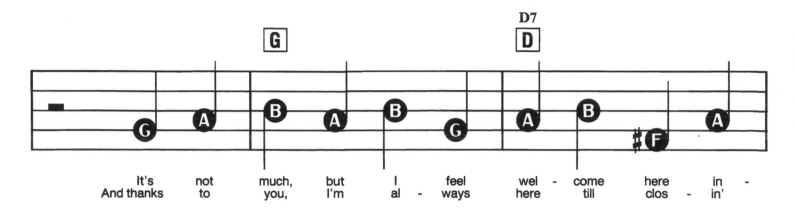

It's not much, but I feel wel - come here in -
And thanks to you, I'm al - ways here till clos - in'

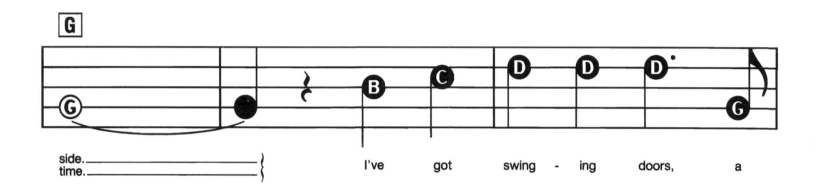

side.
time.

I've got swing - ing doors, a

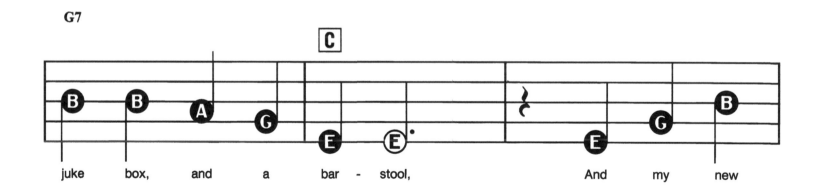

juke box, and a bar - stool, And my new

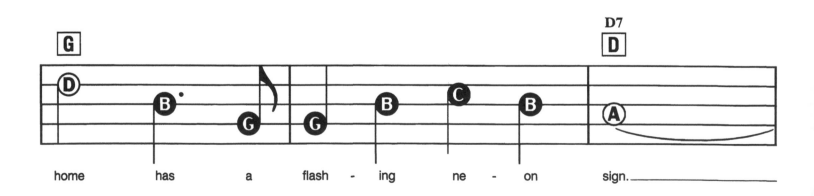

home has a flash - ing ne - on sign.

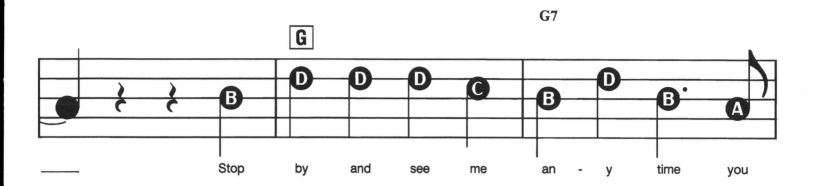

Stop by and see me an - y time you

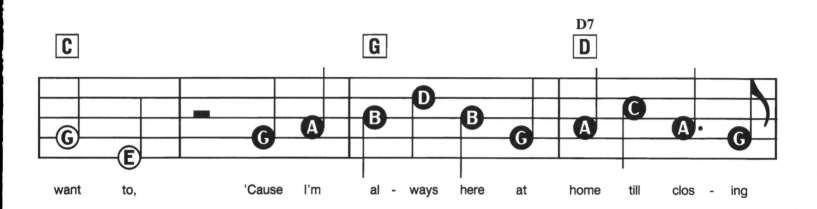

want to, 'Cause I'm al - ways here at home till clos - ing

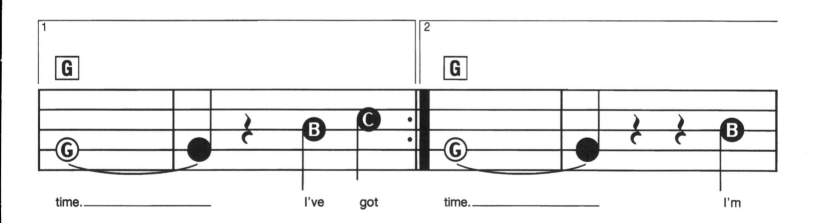

time._____ I've got time._____ I'm

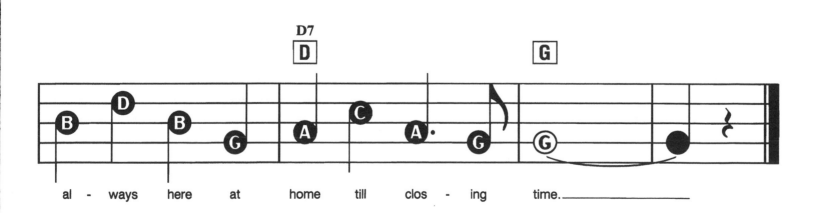

al - ways here at home till clos - ing time._____

# Someday We'll Look Back

Registration 8
Rhythm: Country or Rock

Words and Music by
Merle Haggard

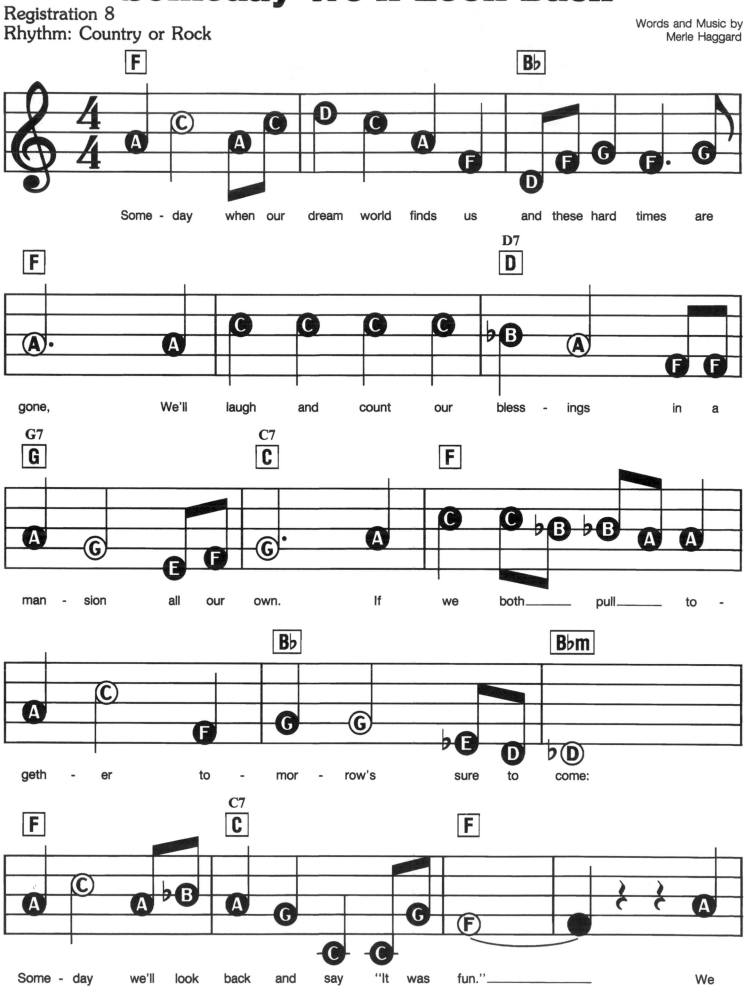

Some - day when our dream world finds us and these hard times are gone, We'll laugh and count our bless - ings in a man - sion all our own. If we both___ pull___ to - geth - er to - mor - row's sure to come: Some - day we'll look back and say "It was fun."_____ We

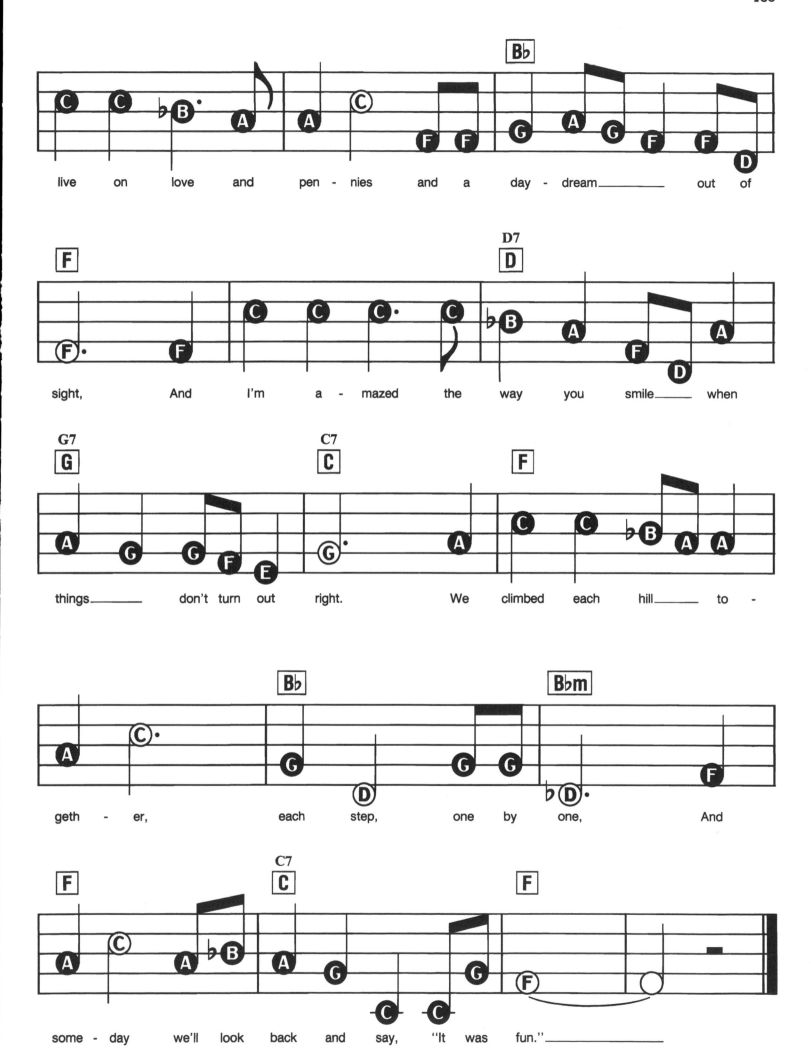

# Twinkle, Twinkle Lucky Star

Registration 1
Rhythm: Rock or Country

Words and Music by
Merle Haggard

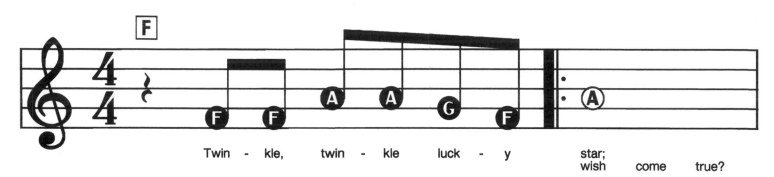

Twin - kle, twin - kle luck - y star;
wish come true?

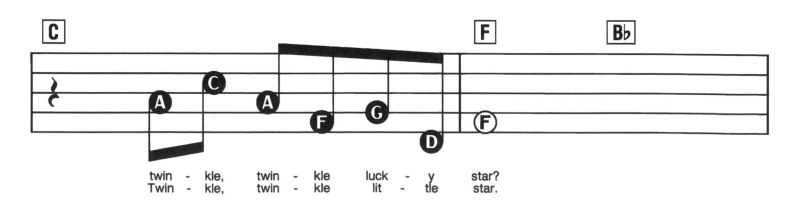

Can you send me luck from where you are?
Do you shine on luck just a few?

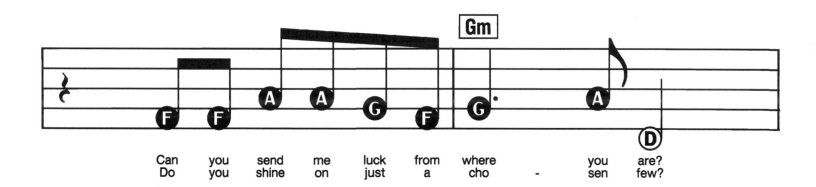

Can you make a rain - bow shine that far,
Is it o - ver; have I gone too far?

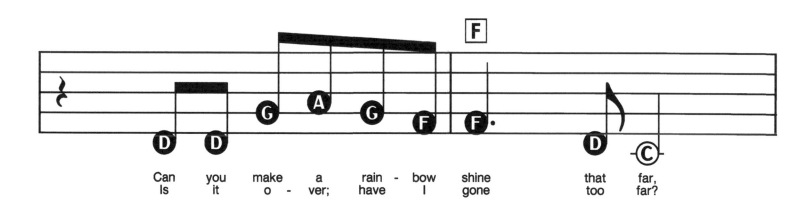

twin - kle, twin - kle luck - y star?
Twin - kle, twin - kle lit - tle star.

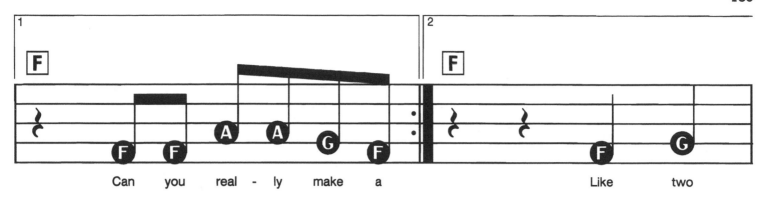

Can you real - ly make a

Like two

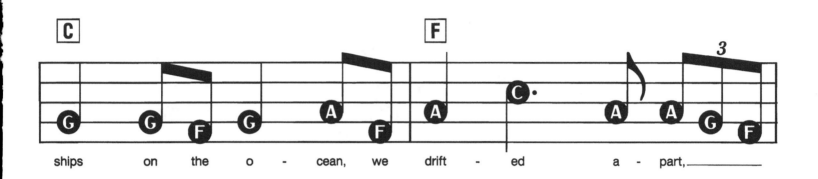

ships on the o - cean, we drift - ed a - part,

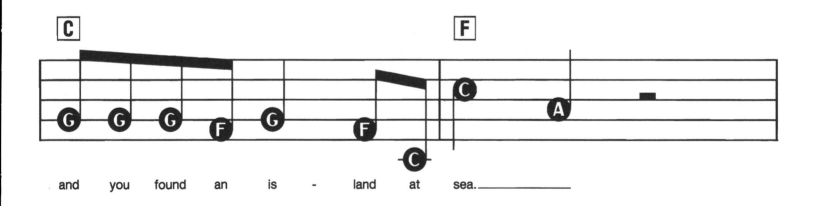

and you found an is - land at sea.

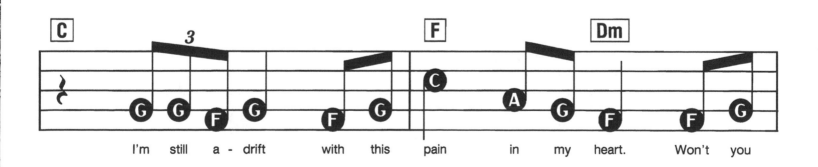

I'm still a - drift with this pain in my heart. Won't you

136

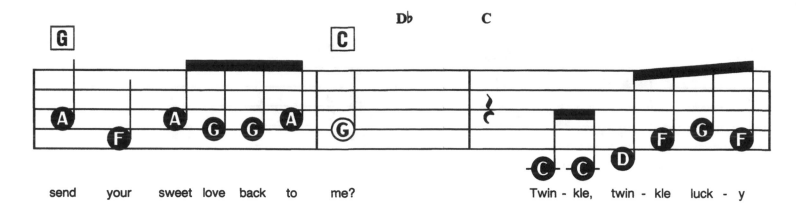

send your sweet love back to me? Twin - kle, twin - kle luck - y

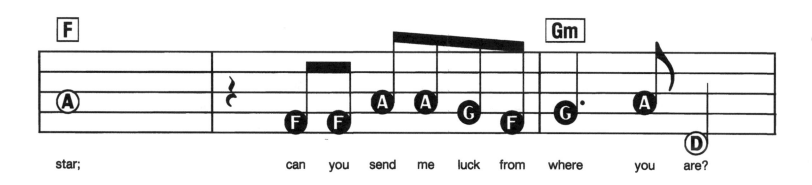

star; can you send me luck from where you are?

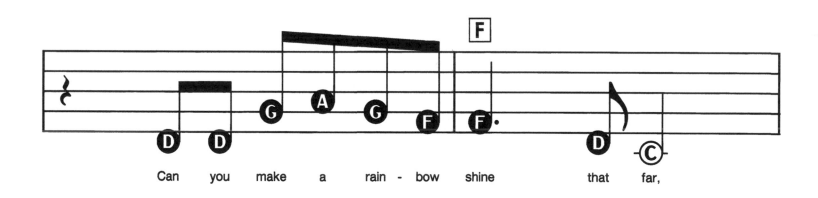

Can you make a rain - bow shine that far,

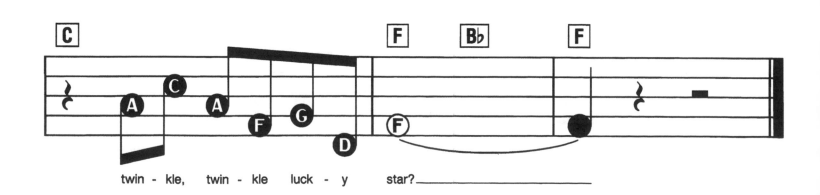

twin - kle, twin - kle luck - y star?_____

# What Am I Gonna Do
## (With The Rest Of My Life)

Registration 7
Rhythm: Country or Ballad

Words and Music by
Merle Haggard

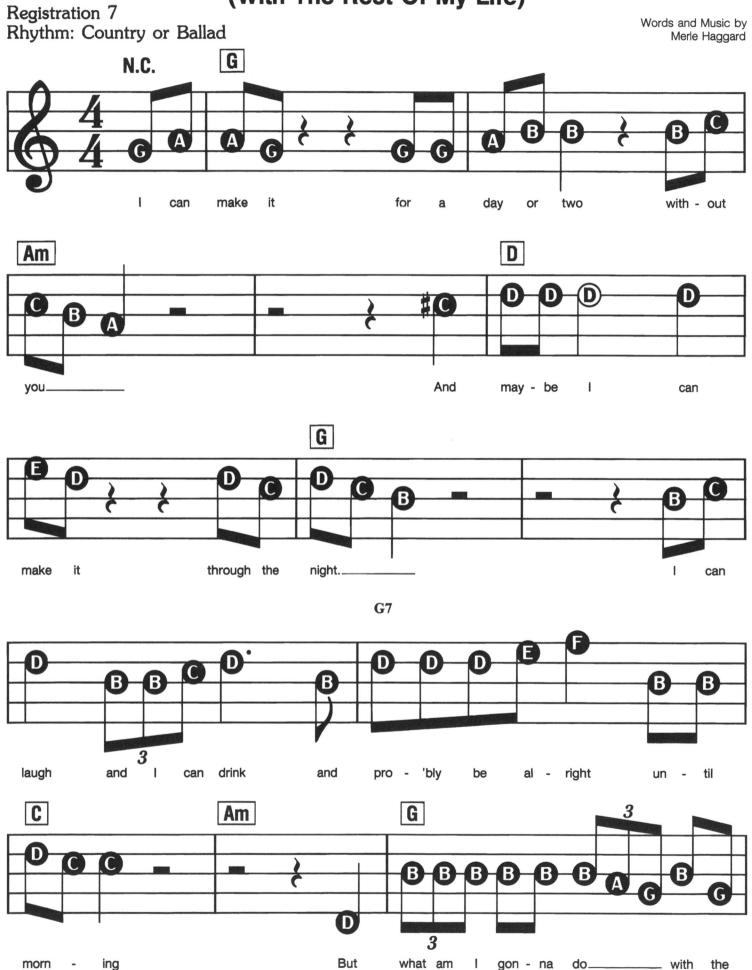

rest of my life? I got

things that I can do. I got plac - es I can go to this
*Instrumental*

eve - ning. I got whis - key I can drink that - 'll

help me not to think a - bout your leav - ing.

G7

Yes, I can smoke and I can drink,

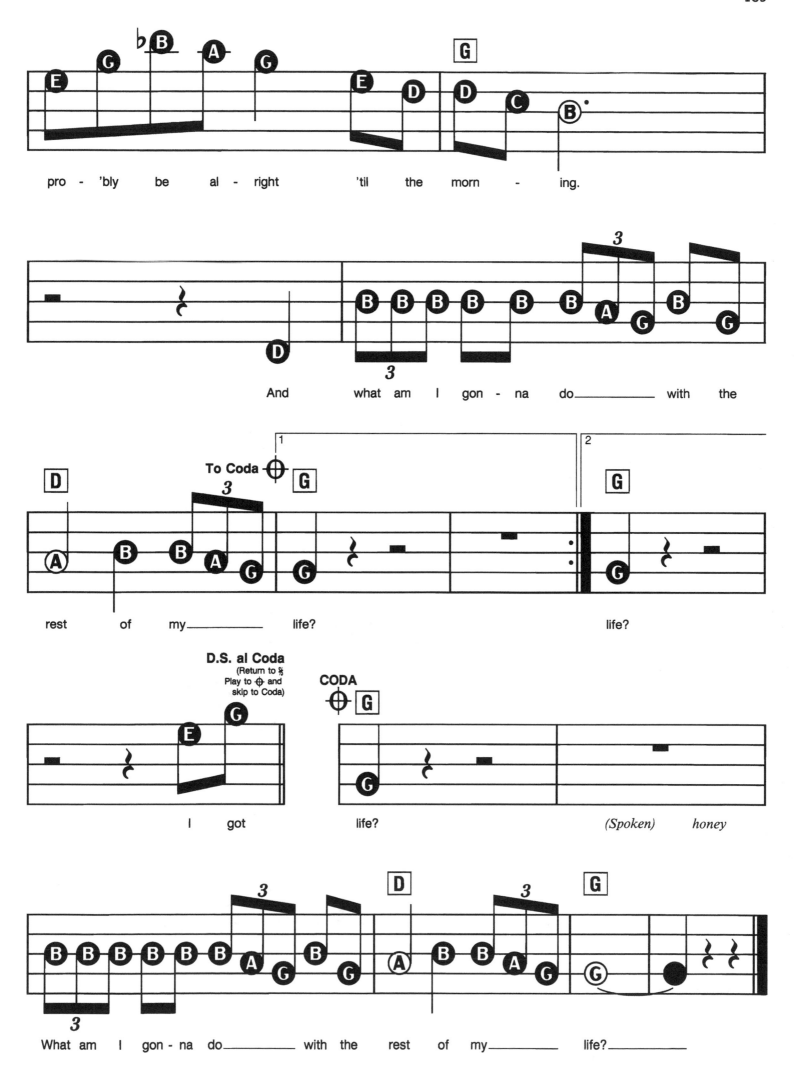

# Workin' Man Blues

Registration 5
Rhythm: Blues or Country

Words and Music by
Merle Haggard

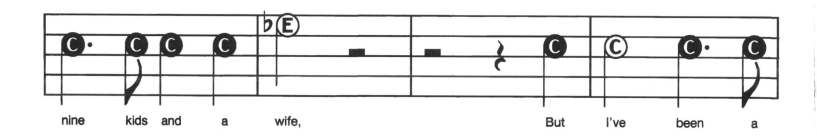

1. It's a big job just get - tin' by with
2-4.(*See additional lyrics*)

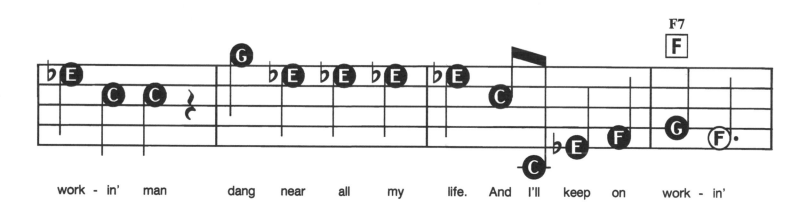

nine kids and a wife, But I've been a

work - in' man dang near all my life. And I'll keep on work - in'

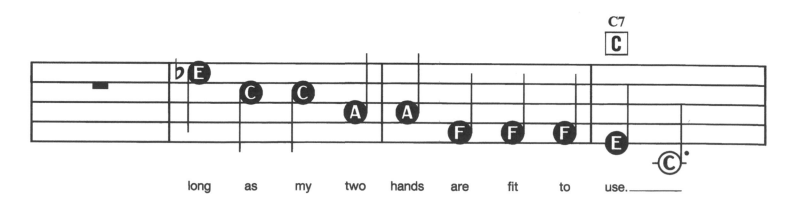

long as my two hands are fit to use.___

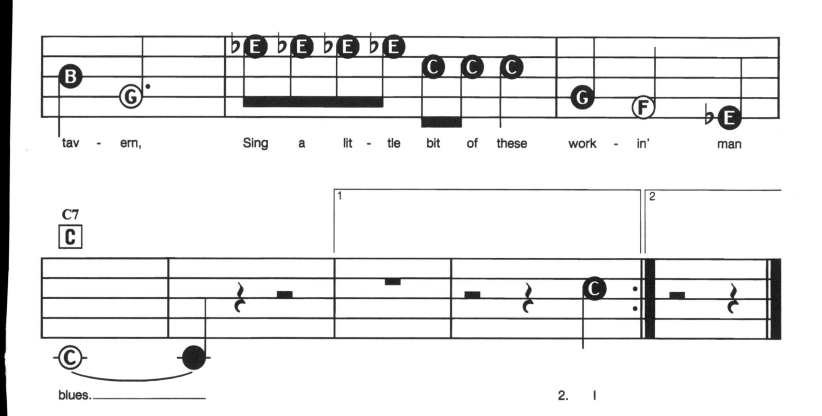

I'll drink my beer in a tav - ern, Sing a lit - tle bit of these work - in' man blues.

2. I

## Additional Lyrics

2. I keep my nose on the grindstone, work hard everyday.
   I might get a little tired on the weekend, after I draw my pay.
   I'll go back workin', come Monday morning I'm right back with the crew.
   And I drink a little beer that evening,
       Sing a little bit of these workin' man blues.

3. Sometimes I think about leaving, do a little bumming around.
   I want to throw my bills out the window, catch a train to another town.
   I'll go back workin', gotta buy my kids a brand new pair of shoes.
   I drink a little beer in a tavern,
       Cry a little bit of these workin' man blues.

4. Well, Hey! Hey! The workin' man, the workin' man like me
   I ain't never been on welfare, that's one place I won't be.
   I'll be workin', long as my two hands are fit to use.
   I'll drink my beer in a tavern
       Sing a little bit of these workin' man blues.

# You Take Me For Granted

Registration 10
Rhythm: Waltz

Words and Music by
Leona Williams

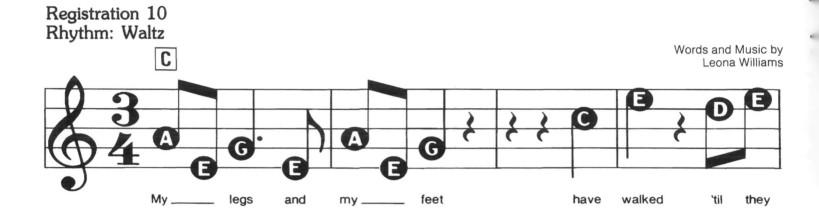

My ____ legs and my ____ feet have walked 'til they

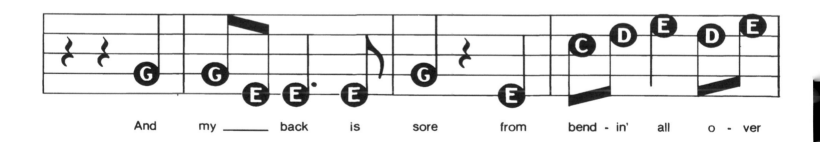

can't hard - ly ____ move from try - in' to please ____ you

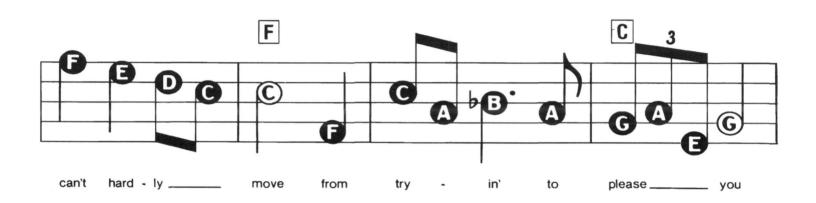

And my ____ back is sore from bend - in' all o - ver

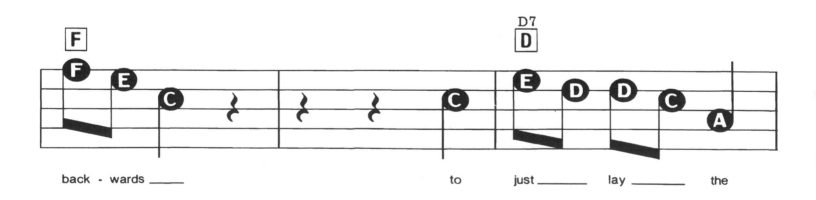

back - wards ____ to just ____ lay ____ the

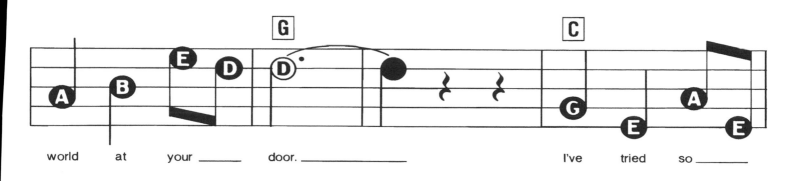

world at your _____ door. _____ I've tried so _____

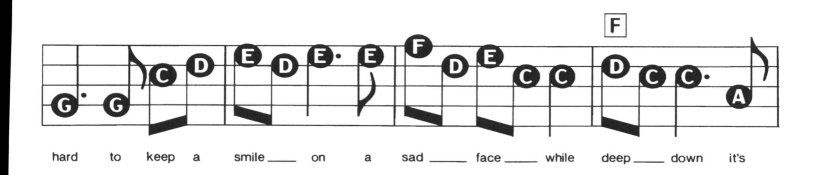

hard to keep a smile____ on a sad ____ face ____ while deep ____ down it's

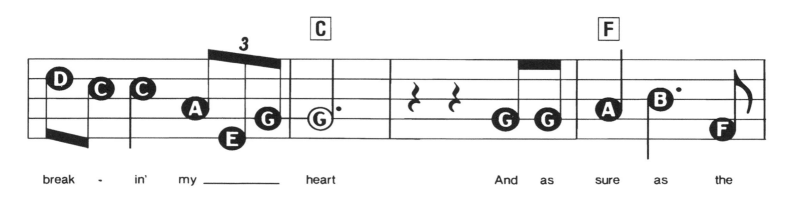

break - in' my _____ heart And as sure as the

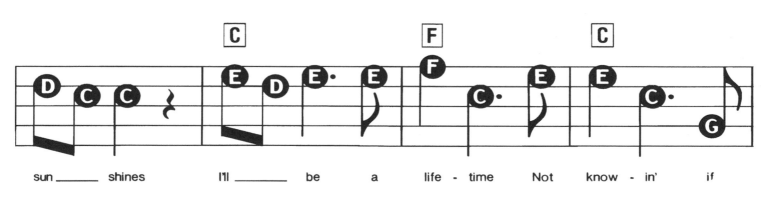

sun ____ shines I'll _____ be a life - time Not know - in' if

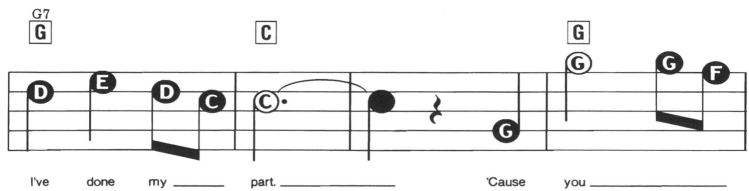

I've done my _____ part. _____ 'Cause you _____

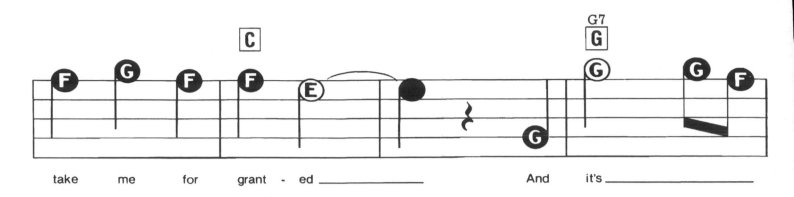

take me for grant - ed _____ And it's _____

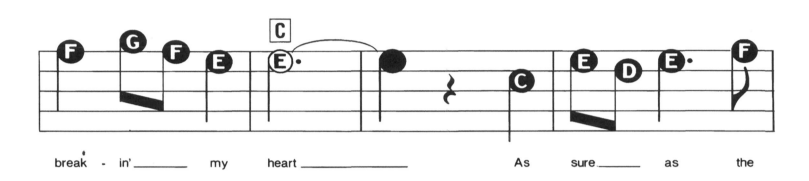

break - in' _____ my heart _____ As sure ____ as the

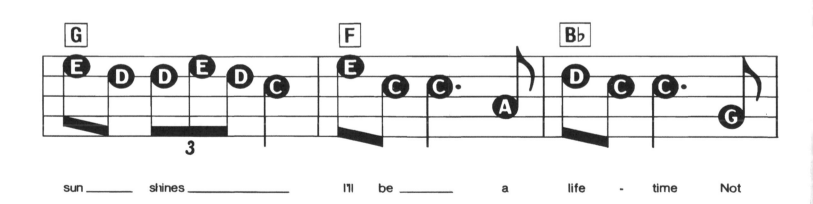

sun ____ shines _____ I'll be ____ a life - time Not

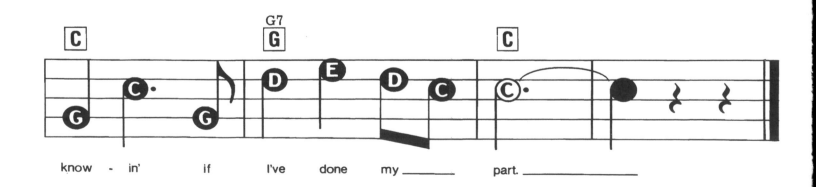

know - in' if I've done my ____ part. _____